# Communication Techniques



**A.P. Girdhar**
*Faculty*
B.K. Birla Institute of Engineering & Technology
Pilani, Rajasthan (India)

**I.K. International Publishing House Pvt. Ltd.**

NEW DELHI • BANGALORE

*Published by*
I.K. International Publishing House Pvt. Ltd.
S-25, Green Park Extension
Uphaar Cinema Market
New Delhi – 110 016 (India)
E-mail: info@ikinternational.com
Website: www.ikbooks.com

ISBN 978-93-82332-24-4



10 9 8 7 6 5 4 3 2 1



Published by Krishan Makhijani for I.K. International Publishing House Pvt. Ltd., S-25, Green Park Extension, Uphaar Cinema Market, New Delhi – 110 016 and Printed by Rekha Printers Pvt. Ltd., Okhla Industrial Area, Phase-II, New Delhi – 110 020.

# Foreword

With an ever increasing need for participation in interactive activities both at the national and international levels, the inculcation of Effective Communication Skills, as part of higher education, has assumed great importance. Responding to the demand of the present-day world many universities have revised the syllabuses of English courses to include those components which could help impart communicative competence.

There are books galore containing teaching materials based on the contents of the revised syllabuses. But keeping in view the variation in the achievement level of students at entry point, some universities prefer to use material, specially produced to meet the specific needs of their students without, of course, compromising with the expected academic standard. The present volume by Prof. A.P. Girdhar is a laudable attempt in this direction. He has discussed the basics of communication and included material for practice in the application of principles of communication in real-life situations. Keeping in mind the needs of students coming through the regional medium school system, he has also provided a section on English grammar and usage.

However, what makes the work unique is the step-by-step explanation of theoretical concepts in plain English. The treatment of each topic is marked by clarity of thought and lucidity of expression. The learner-centred, easy-to-understand style of presentation adds further value to the book, making it suitable for professionally-oriented courses in English. Undoubtedly it is a valuable addition in the area of English communication. I believe the book would receive a quick and favourable response from the target audience.

**Krishna Mohan**
Formerly Professor of English
Birla Institute of Technology and Science
Pilani

# Preface

The present age is characterized by speed, efficiency and competition. The world has witnessed great complexity in organizational and individual behaviour in recent years. There has been rapid industrial growth which has necessitated revolutionary changes in business management techniques. This has its impact on communication techniques. There has been greater realization about the importance of communication skills. It is commonly believed that ability to communicate effectively is the key to the success of a business venture.

The inculcation of communication skills has assumed great importance with the universities. They have revised their syllabuses to include courses on communication techniques in almost every discipline of academics to meet the requirements of business organizations. In consequence a number of books on communication techniques are available in the market. This book has been specially designed to explain the fundamentals of the various aspects of communication in the simplest possible language. Simplicity of language is the greatest strength of this book.

The book is divided into five units. The first unit explains the meaning, importance and process of communication. It also explains the objectives of communication, as well as media and types of communication.

Part II of the book has chapters on phonetic transcription and vocabulary building.

The second unit describes verbal and non-verbal communication, formal and informal channels of communication and qualities of good communication.

The third unit explains the barriers to communication, professional communication, interpersonal communication and how to improve it.

To enable the students to express their ideas clearly in grammatically correct English some important grammatical topics like subject-verb agreement, linking words, relative pronoun have been discussed in Unit 4. This unit also includes some common errors which are usually committed by Indian students with explanation of the rules of grammar to rectify these errors.

The fifth unit deals with composition laying particular emphasis on resume writing, writing of business letters, e-mails and telephone etiquettes.

It is hoped that the book will prove useful to students and will find a favourable response.

**A.P. GIRDHAR**

# Acknowledgements

The author of a book often needs some motivation, encouragement and support for writing the book. Naturally he/she feels indebted to those persons who provide this support. For this kind of support and encouragement I am indeed very grateful to Dr. P.S. Bhatnagar, Director, B. K. Birla Institute of Engineering Technology, Pilani. It is not always possible to express one's true feelings of gratitude in words. One finds oneself quite unequal to the task of expressing one's true feelings and this is also true of me.

I am equally indebted to Prof. Krishna Mohan, formerly Professor of English at Birla Institute of Technology and Science, Pilani who has provided his most valuable guidance in preparing this book. His suggestions have helped me a lot and I shall always remain grateful to him.

I am thankful to the two Deans of the Institute, Prof. S.B. Dandin and Prof. L. Solanki for their kind support and encouragement from time to time.

My thanks are also due to my great friends Dr. S.R. Yadav, Dr. Vipin Kumar, Dr. A. K. Malik and Ms. Ruchi for their kind support.

**A.P. GIRDHAR**

# Contents



## PART - I

### UNIT 1 - ELEMENTS OF COMMUNICATION



### UNIT 2 - BASICS OF COMMUNICATION



### UNIT 3 - SKILLS OF COMMUNICATION

# PART I

UNIT 1

# Elements of Communication

1. Communication: Meaning, Importance and Process
2. Objectives of Communication
3. Media and Types of Communication

# 1

# Communication: Meaning, Importance and Process

**LEARNING OBJECTIVES**

- To understand the meaning of communication and its importance.
- To know the process of communication and elements of communication.

## MEANING

Communication means to communicate. It means to express and convey ideas, opinions, feelings, etc. The activity or process of expressing ideas and feelings is called communication. It means sharing of information. Communication skills means our ability or skill to convey our thoughts and ideas to others. It is an essential requirement for all human interactions. It is a process of exchange of ideas, opinions and information. Communication is not confined to messaging or sharing of information. It involves not just words but the use of all our senses. In face-to-face conversation, facial expressions, tone, body language, ability to listen with patience play an important role.

Communication is a general phenomenon. Communication takes place everywhere. The world cannot exist without some sort of communication. We have no choice but to communicate. Even if we try to avoid communicating with some people on some occasions by not replying to them, it is still a sort of communication. Of course, it will not amount to effective communication.

Communication is not confined to human beings only. All the creatures including birds, animals, insects communicate but they have their own ways of communicating. Birds, animals and insects produce various kinds of sounds to communicate. They also use body language to communicate. A dog waves its tail in the air to communicate its sense of gratitude to its master. It barks to communicate its anger. But man is the only creature who has developed highly scientific languages as the main source of communication.

## ORIGIN OF COMMUNICATION

Communication started in the life of man as soon as life began on this earth. A baby starts communicating as soon as it is born though it does not know the language. It cries when hungry. It smiles to convey its happiness. It has its own ways of expressing its satisfaction, anger, approval, etc.

## IMPORTANCE OF COMMUNICATION SKILLS

Man is a social being and communication has always been very important in social life. But communication skills have acquired great importance in the modern world. The modern age is characterized by speed and efficiency. It has the ability to transcend physical and geographical limitations. We live in an age where effective communication has acquired great importance. The process of communication may be as old as the universe itself but the rapid technical and scientific advancement of the world has enormously increased the importance of effective communication skills and their scope. Now mobiles, computers and the Internet have become the most favoured means of communication.

Business communication is a specialized branch of communication. But there is no basic difference between business communication and general communication. The process involved in both these kinds of communication is the same. Business communication deals with some special business activities and it is formal in nature. General communication has wider roles to play in social life and it may be formal or informal.

## ADVANTAGES OF EFFECTIVE COMMUNICATION

The rapid scientific and technological advancements in today's world require effective skills of communication. Some of the advantages of effective communication are:

1. No organization can function effectively without an effective communication process. Its success depends on the ability of its manpower to interact effectively. Good communication skills help in building better relationships both at the personal level and at the official level.
2. In this age of globalization business houses and government offices have to deal with people of different cultures and languages which requires the ability to communicate effectively.
3. Every organization aims at expansion of its activities. The coordinator of the whole affair requires effective communication skills.
4. In recent times management style has changed from all management to participative management. Its success depends on the effectiveness of communication skills.
5. We are living in a highly competitive business world. Success in such competitive environment depends on effective communication skills.
6. Business houses are paying more and more attention to human relations. It depends on the skilful use of communication techniques.
7. Good and skilful communication can ease the tension between two warring nations and help in establishing better relationship between them.
8. Good communication skills minimize the gap among various departments in an organization. This improves

understanding and promote relationships thereby improving efficiency of the organization.

9. At the personal level the ability to communicate well builds confidence and self-esteem of an individual.

## ELEMENTS OF COMMUNICATION

There are several elements of communication. The first element of communication is the content or the idea to be conveyed by the sender of the message. The second element is called the encoding of the message/idea. Then there is the channel through which the message is transmitted. The fourth is the reception of the message. The fifth is the decoding of the message. The understanding of the decoded message is the sixth element of communication. The seventh is the feedback that the receiver sends. It is a sign of confirmation that the message has been received.

Even 'noise' may also be considered an element of communication. It is a negative element because it creates interruption in the process of communication.

## PROCESS OF COMMUNICATION

Any communication process involves two persons or two parties - the one who addresses (sender) and the addressee (the receiver). The communication will not be complete if the message conveyed by the sender is not understood properly by the receiver.

The communication will be successful only if the sender and receiver share some common background, common purpose, common interests and common channel of communication. So the speaker has to make a choice of symbols and the kind of language which are understood by the receiver of the communication. The language and symbols change as the situation warrants and according to the person one is speaking to. When one is talking to a group of scientists one has to use scientific terminology and dignified language but if the same person is talking to his wife at home he will use simple and colloquial language.

The following elements are involved in the process of communication:

### Sender (Encoder)

The most important element of a communication process is the sender. He is responsible for sending the message. He is also called the encoder. He puts the message into words or images. He must encode his message taking into consideration the receiver's social background, intellectual level and competence in the language used.

### Receiver (Decoder)

The receiver is the person or a group of persons who receive the message. The receiver of the message is also called the decoder. He decodes the message, i.e., he interprets and translates the message. If the message does not reach the receiver or it is not properly understood by the receiver, the process of communication has failed.

### The Topic (Message)

Another important element of communication is the topic, i.e., the content of the message. The purpose of a communication is the sending of a message. It can be an idea, feeling or some information. In business communication every communication has a purpose. Its purpose is to accomplish something by communicating.

### The Channel

The channel is the medium through which the message is transmitted from one person to another. The channel must be appropriate. Messages may be communicated through the language shared by the sender and the receiver. It may be English, French, Hindi or any other language shared by the sender and the receiver. The communication will be successful if the one who addresses and the one who is addressed share the common language.

### Feedback

When a message is received by the receiver, he/she reacts to the message. Through his/her reaction the sender knows whether the receiver has received and understood the message properly or not. Often feedback is in the form of return of a portion of the message as an acknowledgement. It may contain some new information. Feedback is very important to make the communication effective. It assures the sender that his/her message has been received and understood properly. If the feedback shows that the message has not been received or understood properly, the sender can take remedial steps.

The entire process of communication takes place within a common frame of reference. It is called communication environment. The source means point of origin of a message. It is encoded by the sender. It is transmitted through the channel to the receiver. The receipt of the message leads to some result. The achievement of the result determines the success of a communication.

The following figure illustrates the process of communication.

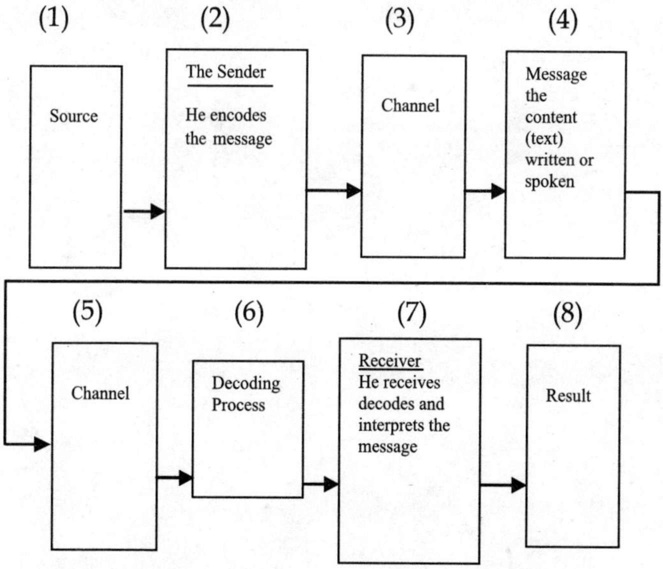

## QUESTIONS FOR DISCUSSION

1. What do you understand by communication? Write a note about its origin and scope.
2. Discuss the importance of effective communication skills in the modern world.
3. What are the elements of communication?
4. Explain the process of communication.

# 2

# Objectives of Communication

**LEARNING OBJECTIVES**

- To know the main objectives of communication.
- To understand the importance of macro objectives of communication.

## OBJECTIVES/FUNCTIONS OF COMMUNICATION

Communication is the basic need not only of human beings but also of all living creatures. We engage in communication as soon as we are born. When we interact with each other we are communicating. We need to communicate in our personal life, social life and for business purposes.

It is not only through words that we communicate. We use all our senses in our communication. During face-to-face conversation our facial expressions, tone, body language contribute to our communication. Even ability to listen with patience contributes to communication.

The ability to communicate well has always been important for human beings but with vast strides in the field of science and technology, its importance and scope have increased greatly.

Communication is more than just communicating messages. It is more than swapping information. The written words in books, magazines, e-mails convey more than just the writing. They can inspire, elevate, and encourage if the writer so intends. The main objective of communication is to communicate. It is an interaction among people for exchange of facts, feelings but objectives of communication are diverse. These objectives are called macro objectives. Some of these objectives are discussed below.

### The Emotive Objective

One of the objectives of communication is to reveal the inner state of the mind and emotions of the speaker. Through communication we express not only the physical needs but also our emotive needs. We express our emotions of love, hatred, compassion, pity, jealousy, etc. We express these emotions and passions not only through words but also through facial expressions and body language. We also utter certain words or expressions to convey our feelings of joy, sorrow, surprise, etc. We speak the word 'alas' to express our grief. The word 'hurrah' is uttered to express our happiness or approval. Political leaders use verbal language and facial expressions to excite the emotions of their audience. Teachers use their communication skills to motivate and encourage their students. Generals of the army use communication techniques to exhort their soldiers to fight bravely and courageously.

### The Directive Objective

Communication also seeks to affect the behaviour of others. Communication is also used to give directions, instructions, commands, etc. If the speaker says "Stand there" he is affecting the behavior of the listener. Imperative sentences are used for this purpose. They seek to affect the behaviour of others. Not only the spoken language but body language is also used to affect the behaviour of others. If we want somebody to stop we raise our hand to give him directions to stop. We can also use the movement of hands to permit somebody to go.

### The Phatic Objective

Communication performs the phatic objective also. The word phatic means "language used for social purposes rather than for seeking information or asking questions". Often we use language for social objectives rather than for giving information or asking questions. Some words are used to open the channel of communication. We make some introductory remarks for opening the channel of communication. Before starting our address we say "Can you hear me", or we may say "Please pay attention". The phatic objective of communication is to arrest the attention of the listeners and prepare them for the address.

### The Poetic Objective

Communication also performs aesthetic objective. There is charm in language. Some writers and speakers use charming expressions in their writings and speeches. It is more so in spoken language where the speaker can use his tone, facial expressions and body language to charm the listeners. Lucidity of diction and spontaneity of expression charm us, emotional utterances touch our hearts, they excite our imagination; create most sensitive and nicest feelings. Poetry, or any kind of literature for that matter, fulfils the aesthetic objective of communication. It expresses man's loftier thoughts and sweet emotions. It moves us to a higher level of consciousness. It fills us with delight and wisdom. Even prose, or day-to-day intercourse, may have the sweetness of poetry.

### The Contextual Objective

Communication also performs the contextual objective. The word "Context" means the words that come just before a word, phrase or statement and help us to understand the context in which the communication is proceeding.

Communication can also create a particular kind of context. Before starting the meeting the coordinator of the meeting may say "Right, let us start the meeting now". He may say "The agenda of the meeting is before you and now we can start the proceedings of the meeting". In this way he creates a particular context.

### The Referential Objective

For a better understanding of the present situation the speaker has to refer back to the past events, incidents or proceedings. Before starting a meeting it is customary to read the minutes of the previous meeting. They give reference to what points were discussed in that meeting. An agenda for the meeting is sent to the participants much in advance. All this comes under the purview of the referential objective of communication.

## QUESTIONS FOR DISCUSSION

1. Discuss the various objectives of communication.
2. Describe the emotive, directive, phatic and poetic objectives of communication.

# 3

# Media and Types of Communication

## LEARNING OBJECTIVES

- To understand the concept of media.
- To understand the various types of communication—verbal and non-verbal.

## INTRODUCTION

Media means the ways through which a large number of people receive information and entertainment, i.e., television, radio, newspaper, the Internet, etc. Communication techniques have been assuming great importance in recent years because of rapid strides in the field of science and technology. Business houses, political parties and social organizations and institutions use various forms of media for the spread of vital information about the important aspects of their activities products or services. Through newspapers, radios, television and the Internet they reach, a great number of persons quickly. In television broadcasts they mix information with entertainment to attract more and more viewers. Political parties use these media for the purpose of propagating their ideas and for communicating agenda of the work they promise to do.

Communication can be classified into the following categories:

1. Written communication
2. Oral communication
3. Gestural communication
4. Visual communication
5. Audiovisual communication
6. Computer based communication
7. Formal and informal communication

## WRITTEN AND GESTURAL MEDIA OF EXPRESSION

Communication can be achieved through writing, speech, gestures and actions. Some people use written words to transmit messages. In schools some teachers draw pictures on the blackboard to explain the meaning of words. One can also use speech sounds. Speech came first into man's life and the writing system was developed much later. We can say that speech is primary and writing is secondary.

Speech is much more used than writing. There are many persons who use speech for communication but they cannot read or write. There may still be some languages which are spoken but have no written forms. If you go to tribal areas, you will find that several of the tribal languages do not have any script. Deaf and dumb persons do not have the faculty of speech. They also communicate but they communicate through actions. But their communication is limited to gestures only. They communicate with ordinary people. They use commonly understood gestures. If they are hungry they take their hands to their mouths to show their need for food.

Writing is the most popular form of communication. In business offices letters, circulars, telegrams, memorandums are written for the purpose of communication. Where wider circulation is necessary, they use newsletters, brochures, bulletins, manuals, reports, magazines, etc.

Oral communication is also used in business transactions. Quite often communication is made through speech. Speech is used in face-to-face interactions, telephone conversations, lectures, talks, meetings and discussions.

We also express our thoughts through body language. It is known as gestural communication. If we have to say 'yes' we move our heads up and down. Nodding of the head from side to side communicates 'no'. We wave our hands in the air to say 'goodbye'. Gestural communication is very useful when there are interruptions of sound or when we are interacting with a person standing at a place where he cannot hear us.

## VISUAL COMMUNICATION

Nowadays visual aids are being used very effectively as a means of communication. Visual means are connected with seeing or sight. In addition to written communication, oral communication, gestural communication, visual aids are being used as means of communication. In schools and colleges, teachers use visual aids such as tables, charts, graphs, diagrams, posters, slides, etc. for communicating. Use of visual communication is not limited to schools and colleges. It is used effectively wherever teaching of principles, transmission of ideas or explanation of concepts are required. Communication through visual aids leaves a lasting impact on the people.

## AUDIO-VISUAL COMMUNICATION

Audio-visual communication combines visual impact with narration. With globalization and with the advent of multinationals video conferences have become the most favoured form of communication.

Audio-visual aids have brought a revolution in the spread of education and information. A great number of schools and colleges are using audio-visual aids in classrooms. Universities like Indira Gandhi Open University are using audio-visual technology through television broadcasts. Students living in towns and remote villages can learn through lectures delivered by highly qualified experts.

## COMPUTER-BASED COMMUNICATION

Today we have the facility of computer based communication. Not only business houses and government offices but individuals also find it easy and economical to communicate through the internet, e-mails and cellular phones. Communication through computer based devices is cheap and quick and one can get instant response.

## CHANNELS OF COMMUNICATION

There are two types of communication channels through which information passes from one side to another. They are formal and informal channels. A network is created in the organization which is responsible for the smooth flow of information. Upward, downward and horizontal information flows through this network.

## FORMAL CHANNELS OF COMMUNICATION

### Downward Communication

Companies have to communicate with other organizations and government offices. They also communicate within the company. If there is a communication between a superior and a subordinate within the company, it is called downward communication. This communication is from higher to lower level of authority. This information may be about the issue of instructions, explanation of policies and practices. It may contain instructions about what to do and when to do? It may be about the feedback to subordinates or such other matters.

### Upward Communication

Communication also flows from subordinates to higher authorities. It may be in the form of a report, suggestion, proposal or a charter of demands from the workers. This kind of communication is called upward communication. Upward communication is important because it provides an outlet to the subordinate staff to express their grievances. It also provides an opportunity to the subordinates to make suggestions and express their opinions about the functioning of the organization and thereby ensure their involvement with the activities of the company.

### Horizontal or Lateral Channel of Communication

If there is communication between officers of the same level of management in the same organization it is called horizontal or lateral communication. It may involve an interaction between Manager (Production) and Manager (Marketing) of the same organization. It may involve exchange of information, ideas or opinions on matters of interest to the organization.

### Diagonal Communication

It is a communication between two officers of different levels in the same organization. Suppose an Assistant Manager in the Credit Department communicates directly with the Regional Manager of the Production Department it is a case of diagonal or crosswise communication.

## INFORMAL CHANNELS OF COMMUNICATION

Some of the needs of an organization may not be fulfilled by the formal channels of communication. Then employees resort to informal talks or discussions. They form friendships and talk in gatherings. Of course such channels of communication are not very reliable. The messages may get distorted and the responsibility for the distortion cannot be fixed. Yet this kind of informal exchange of ideas has some advantages. It fulfils the social needs. It also establishes better relationship among employees of the organization. Some of the sources of informal channel are:

1. Social gatherings provide occasions for informal exchange of ideas, opinions, etc.
2. Often managers make a round of the workplace. During these visits they make informal talks with the

workers. This serves as a means of informal exchange of ideas.

## GRAPEVINE

Grapevine means an informal way of talking to other people. People hear a lot of things through gossips and rumours. It serves as a very useful channel of communication. It is a widespread network of communication. It is outside the formal channel of communication.

## FEATURES AND IMPORTANCE OF GRAPEVINE

1. Grapevine is related to social and personal interaction of the employees
2. Grapevine communication is oral in nature
3. Grapevine communication spreads very fast.
4. The transmission of information is widespread and it spreads in all directions.
5. Grapevine activity increases with the growth and development of the organization.

## HOW DOES GRAPEVINE FUNCTION?

1. Grapevine functions in many different ways. In one such case A may tell something to B and B may tell the same thing to C. In the process the information may get distorted. So the accuracy of this channel of communication cannot be relied upon.
2. Sometimes a person in an organization has got some information and passes on this information to everyone. This is called the gossip chain of communication.
3. In some cases some information is conveyed to some few selected persons. These few selected persons pass on this information to some other few selected persons. This pattern of communication is more popular. It is called cluster chain of communication.
4. Sometimes information is passed on at random. It does not matter as to whom the information is passed on.

This kind of communication is called probability chain of communication.

## QUESTIONS FOR DISCUSSION

1. Define media and types of communication.
2. Discuss the various categories into which media communication can be categorised.
3. Describe oral communication and its importance in business organization.
4. Discuss the importance of (a) written communication (b) gestural communication.
5. Explain briefly:
    a. Upward communication
    b. Downward communication
    c. Horizontal or lateral communication
6. Describe the features of:
    a. Formal communication
    b. Informal communication.

UNIT 2

# Basics of Communication

# 4

# Verbal and Non-verbal Communication

## LEARNING OBJECTIVES

- To understand the various types of communication – verbal and non-verbal
- To understand the nature of oral and written forms of communication
- To learn the nature of non-verbal forms of communication like body language, sign language, gestures, etc.

## INTRODUCTION

To communicate is the basic need of all creatures on this earth. Creatures use various kinds of sounds and gestures to communicate. Man has developed a highly skilful and complex system of language to communicate. For human beings language is the most important tool of communication. It has spoken and written forms. Communication through language is called verbal form of communication. Man also communicates through gestures and body language. This is called non-verbal form of communication. People often combine non-verbal form of communication with verbal communication to make it more effective.

## VERBAL COMMUNICATION

What is verbal communication? Verbal means "relating to words". So verbal communication means "communication through words". It may be in the form of written words or spoken words, i.e., written communication and oral communication.

## ORAL COMMUNICATION

Oral communication means communication by way of uttering words, i.e., speaking. Oral communication is used more than written communication. It is the fastest type of communication. Oral communication reveals the gender, age and geographical background of the speaker. From the oral communication we may also come to know the level of education of the speaker as well as his/her emotional state. Oral communication is used in the meetings and conferences of organizations and government offices. It is also used in face-to-face conversations and telephone conversations.

Oral communication came first in the life of man. Written communication came much later. In oral communication the speaker is face-to-face with the listener. He/she can monitor and match the reactions of the listener. In oral communication the speaker can use gestures, the feature which is denied in written communication.

### Advantages of Oral Communication

1. Oral communication ensures the personal attention of the listener.
2. It is economical and more effective.
3. No records of oral communication are kept. So it remains confidential.
4. Even illiterate persons communicate through oral communication.
5. In the case of oral communication one gets instant feedback and can express one's reactions. One can also seek instant clarifications and clear his doubts.

6. In cases where immediate action is required it is better to transmit a message orally.
7. Oral communication is very helpful when one has to communicate with a large number of people, i.e., assemblies, meetings, etc.
8. Oral communication is carried on the informal plane. It promotes friendly relationship between the two parties.

### Disadvantages of Oral Communication

1. Written communication has documentary proof. Oral communication has no documentary proof or record of the proceedings. We cannot refer back to it.
2. If the oral communication is between persons living far away from each other it is quite expensive.
3. Oral communication is not suitable for complex or lengthy messages.
4. It generates physical noise.
5. Oral communication has greater chances of getting misunderstood, because of the variations in spoken language and the way it is delivered.
6. Oral messages have no legal validity.
7. Speech is far less organized in comparison to written language. It has many incomplete sentences.

## WRITTEN COMMUNICATION

Language is a tool of communication. It has spoken and written forms. These forms serve the same purpose but their forms and manners are different. One makes the use of sounds, the other makes the use of symbols. While using the oral communication the speaker has the full range of voice quality effects which are denied in the case of written communication.

Written communication is much more used in business organizations and government offices. Messages are communicated through various forms of written communication like memorandums, business letters, circulars and notices. In the case of written communication the writer has a lot of time at his/her disposal to plan his/her communication to ensure that it is clear, complete, correct and easy to understand.

### Advantages of Written Communication

1. Written communication provides permanent record for future references.
2. The writer has enough time to plan, write or rewrite, what he wants to communicate. So it is complete, precise and unambiguous.
3. It can be referred back again. It can be read and re-read till it is properly understood.
4. Written communication is very useful when it is meant for a large number of people. The message can be circulated to a large number of people and it can be repeated if necessary.
5. It serves as a legal document.

### Disadvantages of Written Communication

1. Written communication is time consuming. It takes a lot of time to draft a document or a letter and get it typed and dispatched.
2. It is expensive.
3. It is difficult to maintain the secrecy of written communication.
4. It has no scope for immediate feedback.

## NON-VERBAL COMMUNICATION

We communicate not only through the use of words. We often communicate without using the formal language made of sounds and words. We use non-verbal channels of communication. A great deal of our communication is in non-verbal form. We spend a lot of our time communicating our ideas, opinions and thoughts to others. Most of it is in non-verbal form.

In the non-verbal channels of communication we use facial expressions, eye-contact, and body language. We also use postures of the body, motion of limbs as forms of non-verbal communication. During a conversation one raises one's eyebrows to express disbelief at a statement. One smiles to welcome a friend. One may wave his/her hand to say good-bye to a friend. Gestures are also used by babies, animals and other creatures to communicate. We communicate through non-verbal means of communication very effectively.

Some of the non-verbal channels of communication are discussed below.

### Personal Appearance

Personal appearance is the most important feature of one's personality. It makes a significant impact on the course of conversation. Personal appearance makes the first and sometimes an everlasting impression and influences the course of negotiations. If a person remains confident and cheerful he/she reveals the strength of his/her character. If one dresses well and conducts oneself gracefully, one makes a good impression and gets motivation and confidence to communicate well.

### Body Language

The use of body language is another important channel of non-verbal communication. In technical parlance it is known as kinesis, i.e., the movement. People use body language for the expression of personal emotions, feelings, attitudes, thoughts, etc. Body language involves gestures, postures, facial expressions, etc. Even walking styles may communicate a lot.

These gestures may be accompanied with verbal communication.

### Facial Expressions

A human face is an open book. The more intelligent the person is, the more intelligently he can read the book of human face. It vividly expresses his/her state of mind. A person can express his/her sense of gratitude or a feeling of happiness and welcome more vividly through a smile than through the utterance of warm words of welcome. A frown can communicate a feeling of anger, outrage and hostility more effectively than words.

There is no emotion which facial expressions cannot convey. They can convey the feelings of love, hatred, anger, confusion, jealousy, etc. But at times facial expressions may not express the feelings truly. A good actor has the ability to hide his/her true feelings and hide his/her evil intentions behind a beguiling smile.

### Eye-movement

It is said that the tongue may lie but the eyes will not. The eyes speak more eloquently than the mouth. When a man is in a mood of reflection, his eyes are partly closed. Restlessness of the mind is revealed by the rolling eyes. If a person avoids eye-contact it shows nervousness. Wide open eyes reveal a feeling of shock. But these revelations through eyes are not uniformly reliable as human nature is varied and there is always some scope of affectation, hypocrisy and wrong judgment.

### Postures

The position of the body while standing or sitting is called posture. The posture communicates a lot about a person's state of mind and his character. It may reveal his level of confidence. It may reveal whether a person is tense or relaxed. If a person is interested in conversation he/she leans forward whereas a bored person repeatedly turns his/her face. A slumped posture conveys low spirits whereas an erect posture shows high level of confidence and energy.

If a man leans forward it shows that he is open-minded and interested. Leaning away shows the defensive attitude as if one is not interested in the conversation. A person standing or sitting with crossed arms shows his defensive frame of mind. The posture of uncrossed arms shows man's willingness to listen.

## Gestures

Gestures are the physical movements that one makes with head and hand to indicate one's reactions, approvals, disapprovals, appreciation or otherwise to some communication. Gestures are spontaneous but one can learn and practise positive gestures to minimize the effect of negative gestures.

### *Positive gestures*

1. Gestures relating to listening and speaking are very important. Leaning forward to listen attentively is a very good gesture. It shows that the listener is interested in the talk. The listener should also maintain eye-contact.
2. Another important gesture is keeping one's hands open and free. Binding of hands or keeping them in pockets is a negative gesture. If one puts one's one hand in pocket it shows his/her arrogance. If one puts both his/her hands in pockets it shows nervousness.
3. One should keep one's head erect while sitting, walking or facing an interview. Even the manner of carrying one's documents is important. There should be grace in it.
4. Often an interview or a business meeting may not proceed smoothly. At such times becoming rude, aggressive, arrogant and negative shows a negative attitude. Maintaining cheerfulness and positive attitude as if nothing has gone wrong at such times helps a lot. This attitude may change the failed interview into a successful one.
5. Positive gestures also involve a state of activeness and alertness. One should not show lack of interest or a state of inertia through body language.

### *Negative gestures*

1. While facing an interview leaning back is a negative gesture. It shows lack of interest.
2. Folding of hands or keeping them in pockets is not a sign of good conduct. It shows lack of graceful manners.
3. Some persons become nervous while facing an interview and start scratching or biting nails. These are negative gestures.
4. Often an interview does not proceed smoothly. At such times losing temper or showing irritation is a negative attitude.
5. Covering the mouth while speaking or glancing sideways is not a sign of good manners.
6. Shaking hands too hard or giving a limp shake hand is a negative gesture.
7. Staring or pointing at someone is a sign of rudeness which one must avoid.
8. Showing of self-importance or becoming rude spoils an interview/meeting.

### Body Shape

How we present our body or the shape of our body during an interaction plays an important role in effective communication. We have no control over our physical appearance but we can adopt the right kind of posture and can improve the impact of our physical appearance.

Standing up tall shows you in a more authoritative position. A bent posture or drooping shoulders reveal a state of passiveness or submissiveness.

### Dress

It is said that dress reveals the man. Dressing well shows your good taste and makes a good impression during an interview/meeting.

One should not wear gaudy clothes during the course of an interview or meeting. Dress must be complete. If a person is wearing a suit it must be accompanied with a neck-tie and he/she must wear shoes and not sandals.

### Smell and Touch

Smell and touch can also influence the course of communication. A man who smells bad may not be welcomed at the time of interview. The interviewers may not say anything directly but may try to avoid him. People use perfumes to avoid bad smell. But too much use of perfumes is also irritating.

A touch is a very good way of showing affection, love and intimacy. It can also convey a feeling of friendliness. A friendly pat on the shoulder of an employee by the manager can go a long way in motivating and enthusing him.

### Modulation of the Voice

Well spoken language has a charm. Good speakers of a language can charm the listeners and thereby make the communication more effective. Well chosen words - words which have lucidity, spoken with correct pronunciation and with correct intonation can charm the listeners. Some people speak in a monotone voice. Listeners find it dull and boring and lose interest in the conversation. If the voice of the speaker does not modulate people lose interest in it.

English is a rhythm-based language. The speaker has to create that rhythm by alternating the stressed and unstressed sounds and using the correct intonation, i.e., the use of falling, rising sounds that bring the modulation of the voice.

### Silence

Silence is also an important feature of communication. It can create a peaceful situation or may cause irritation depending on the situation. If there is a heated argument and both the parties keep silence for sometime it eases the situation and they may start their negotiations afresh. On the other hand keeping silent and not responding to the querries may cause irritation.

## Visual Symbols

Visual symbols are used to communicate messages, give advice, commands and make requests, etc. Pictures, cartoons, paintings, maps come into the category of visual symbols. Some symbols have common meaning throughout the world. Mathematical symbols, traffic symbols are standard symbols "No Smoking" signs and white flags have also standard meaning. Colours are also used as symbols. White colour symbolizes peace, red colour symbolizes blood and violence. Visual symbols convey a lot in short space and time. Vehicle drivers have no time to stop and read the written instructions. They just look at the symbols for guidance. The sign of a school boy carrying his bag suggests the existence of a school nearby and advises the drivers to be careful and slow down. Similar useful symbols are there for the hospitals and railway crossings. These can be understood even by illiterate persons.

Visual symbols are being used in advertisements and promotional campaigns.

These symbols have their limitations. There is no scope for interpretation. Moreover in the case of some visual signs interpretations depend on the attitude and mental ability of the viewers.

## CONCLUSION

Of course the purpose of communication is to communicate a message precisely, accurately with clarity. But good communication skills do much more than that.

Good communication can create an environment of friendliness, can bring people closer. It can generate happiness besides communicating. A good written message or well spoken words showing good intentions can create a feeling of happiness.

Another test of skilful communication is whether one can say "no" without creating unhappiness and disappointment during a conversation. Often during a conversation one has to disagree and say "no". Whether one can do so without antagonizing the listener is the real test of the ability of the speaker to communicate well. While rejecting a request you can say rudely (1) I cannot accept your request or (2) You may say politely: I am really sorry I am not in a position to accept your request.

## QUESTIONS FOR DISCUSSION

1. Define verbal and non-verbal communication.
2. What is oral communication? What are its advantages and disadvantages?
3. Discuss the advantages and disadvantages of written communication.
4. Discuss the elements of non-verbal communication.
5. Show the importance of the following in communication:
   a. Personal appearance
   b. Body Language
   c. Facial expressions
   d. Eye movement
6. Discuss the positive gestures as a means of communication.
7. Discuss the disadvantages of negative gestures.

# 5

# Formal and Informal Channels of Communication

## LEARNING OBJECTIVES

- To understand formal and informal channels of communication.

## FORMAL COMMUNICATION

A channel of communication is the medium through which messages are communicated in an organization. This channel of communication can be formal or informal.

In a business organization formal process of communication is preferred. If the communication is done through the chain of command it is known as formal communication. It may be the circulation of official messages in the formal organizational structure. It is planned by the management. It is generally in the written form. It communicates orders, decisions, and instructions. It may also lay down job procedures. It may convey instructions. The messages may explain policies and practices or they may give feedback to employees.

Organizations set up formal channels of communication for the smooth and efficient flow of information. Normally messages move in two directions. These movements are called horizontal and vertical. If the messages are to be exchanged among members working at the same level within an organization it is called horizontal channel of communication. In the case of horizontal channel of communication the communication passes on between different departments or divisions in the same organization, may be between the Production Department and Marketing Department of the same organization. There is little chance of communication barrier due to chain of command technique in this kind of communication.

The other channel of communication in the case of formal channel of communication is vertical channel of communication. In this form of communication there are upward and downward channels of communication system. Messages are transmitted to employees. This kind of transmission of messages is known as downward flow of communication. If the messages are passed on from the employees to the management the process is known as upward channel of communication. This upward channel of communication is used for getting feedback from the employees. It is also used for the expression of feelings, complaints or grievances of the employees.

Downward channel of communication is in the form of letters, circulars, memos, notices, etc. Upward messages are in the form of reports, requests, opinions, results of surveys and statistical analysis.

The formal channels of communication often involve delays due to the processing of information through several people. It also involves too many transfer stations resulting in the distortion of the original message. This process of communication should be two-way. If it is restricted to one way it may suffer from lack of coordination. In present times more and more companies are modifying their communication network to ensure direct access from top to bottom and from bottom to top to remove communication barriers. To make the flow of information smooth and to minimize the scope of barriers to communication a large number of companies are disseminating information through several channels. They are also establishing feedback systems to know the opinions, ideas, grievances, aspirations of the employees. The establishment of network of formal channels of communication plays a very important role in the efficient management of an organization.

## INFORMAL CHANNELS OF COMMUNICATION

Informal communication involves free expression of opinions, ideas and reactions. It does not flow through the official channels. It is usually done orally. Formal and informal communications require change of form and language. Informal communication requires the change of language suiting the position of the addresser and addressee. It means one may use informal language when talking to one's wife at home. But when one is talking to one's wife who happens to be an employee in the same organization one will address her in the formal way.

The informal channel of communication depends on the grapevine. Grapevine means talking in an informal way to other people. It involves rumours, gossips, discussions among the employees, exchange of ideas among them about the functioning of the organization. It may be about their grievances, complaints, etc.

Grapevine is a very important channel of communication in organizations. It is the result of common interests of the employees in an organization. If used properly, it can prove very useful.

This channel of communication has great merits. Through this channel people express their views and opinions frankly and independently. Employees form friendship and they talk in gatherings. Such channels are not cent per cent authentic. Sometimes the messages get distorted. In spite of these limitations this kind of channel serves many useful purposes. It can be very helpful in understanding and appreciating the view-point of the people and knowing their grievances, complaints as also their aspirations and expectations from the employers. In this way remedial steps can be taken for the redressal of the grievances of the employees and steps can be taken to meet with their expectations and aspirations.

This kind of channel bridges the gap between employers and employees.

This channel of communication has another merit. It saves a lot of paper work and stationery.

Some of the communication needs of the organizations may not be met by the formal channels of communication. Formal channels of communication are time-consuming. If the message is urgent it is directly addressed to the employees through an address system. This informal channel of communication is very useful in some other cases like:

(1) Addressing social gatherings.
(2) When the managers are on their rounds of the workplace and interact with the workers during the course of their visit.
(3) The transmission is possible to all the directions in the organization.
(4) Process of informal communication establishes an informal and friendly understanding between employers and employees.

## QUESTIONS FOR DISCUSSION

1. Discuss the formal channels of communication highlighting their importance in business organizations.
2. Discuss the importance of informal channels of communication.
3. Discuss the characteristics of grapevine.

# 6

# Qualities of Good Communication

## LEARNING OBJECTIVES

- To learn the qualities of good communication.
- To learn the advantages of good communication.

## INTRODUCTION

The ability to communicate well is the most important feature of a person's personality. The most essential requirement for success in professional life is the ability to communicate well. There are certain qualities which ensure success both in written and oral forms of communication. These qualities are applicable to all forms of communication. Some of these qualities of good communication are discussed below.

## QUALITIES OF GOOD COMMUNICATION

### Clarity

The first quality of good communication is clarity. Clarity means the quality of being expressed clearly. The receiver must understand the meaning of the message exactly as the sender wants to convey. There should be no scope for any doubt, misunderstanding or ambiguity. To achieve this goal the sender must choose precise, concrete and familiar words.

He/she may plan or even write the communication beforehand. He/she is not making a speech to create an impression. His/her aim is to communicate a message precisely and clearly. The sender should construct short sentences. These should be grammatically correct. Unity and coherence in the formation of sentences make the understanding of the message easy.

### Brevity

It is said that brevity is the soul of wit. Brevity means the quality of using few words while speaking or writing. Conciseness is the most important virtue for any kind of communication. The message must be communicated in the fewest possible words. If the message can be conveyed in ten words why should it be conveyed in fifteen or twenty words? If the message is not concise it may create confusion, misunderstanding or ambiguity. It results in the wastage of time of the sender as well as of the receiver. While communicating one should stick to the relevant material. The choice of words is also important. One should choose simple and short words instead of phrases involving many words. One should also take care not to talk or write about obvious things or things which are already known and should avoid repetition.

### Completeness

The communication should be complete in all respects. It must contain all the facts that the receiver wants to know. The sender of the communication should ensure that after receiving the communication the receiver will not need any further information or clarification.

Complete and precise communications build the image and reputation of the company. Incomplete messages tarnish the image of an organization. It also results in the wastage of time and resources.

## Consideration (Empathy)

To be thoughtful about the feelings or wishes of other people is a healthy and positive attitude and it paves the way for smooth and effective communication. The sender's ability to understand the feelings, expectations and reactions of the receiver and giving due consideration to them is an essential feature of good communication. The sender's goodwill and his friendly attitude must find reflection in his/her communication. The sender should lay emphasis on positive and pleasant aspects. He/she should lay emphasis on what can be done and not on what cannot be done.

## Concreteness

A message must have concreteness. It should be based on facts, not on ideas or guesses. It should be definite and not vague.

## Choice of Words

It is better to use denotational words in the message. Denotational words refer to the actual objects or ideas and there is little chance of misunderstanding. Use of connotations suggests various ideas of a word in addition to its main meaning. For example the word 'professional' has connotations of skill and excellence. Use of connotations is good in literature but not in practical matters of life. A connotation suggests a meaning of a word separate from the dictionary meanings of the word and its use may create confusion. If it is necessary to use a connotation the sender must make sure that the receiver is aware of the additional meanings of the connotation. The sender of the message should choose words carefully to make sure that the message has correctness and will not pose any problems of understanding.

## Ability to Listen with Patience

One of the important qualities of a good communication is the receiver's ability to listen with patience. He/she should not be in a hurry to respond. He/she should have patience to listen, think and form his/her response. This is very important in the case of oral communication. In the case of written communication the sender has sufficient time to form his/her response and draft his/her message. But this is not possible in the case of oral communication. So one needs to be extra careful.

### Politeness

Of course, the purpose of any communication is to communicate a message and a good communication must serve this purpose. But a good communication should generate goodwill and friendliness also. A good communication should be a source of pleasure. It should have the ability to generate happiness. To achieve all the above mentioned purposes a communication must have the virtue of extreme courtesy. Politeness is a greatly rewarding virtue. There is never a valid reason for arrogance and ill-temper. Nothing should provoke the speaker to be impolite.

To achieve this objective the sender must be thoughtful and appreciative of the other's point of view. He/she should show genuine consideration and respect to the sender.

## ATTRIBUTES OF THE COMMUNICATORS

In addition to the above-mentioned points the sender of the oral message must have the following attributes:

1. The sender must have clarity of mind to communicate effectively.
2. He/she must speak in simple and straight language to make the message explicit leaving no scope for misunderstanding or confusion.
3. He/she must do homework for making the message precise and concrete.
4. In the case of oral communication body language is very important. The sender must exhibit self-confidence through body language. It is necessary that the sender should fill his/her communication with

enthusiasm and energy. His/her message should show a positive attitude towards life.

5. The sender of the communication must cultivate the ability to arouse interest in the audience.
6. He/she should be able to check filters and barriers to communication.
7. In the case of oral communication the voice quality of the sender matters a lot. He/she should modulate his/her voice by alternating the stressed and unstressed syllables of the speech with accurate pauses to avoid monotony and dullness in the communication of the message.
8. The greatest virtue of the speaker is to remain cheerful during the course of a communication as it reflects his/her confidence. Cheerfulness is infectious. It spreads from the sender to the receiver of the communication. Expression of cheerfulness through a genuine and pleasing smile makes the communication refreshing and charming.
9. During the course of an address one should not stand still at one place. He/she should make a few convenient movements within the available space.

## SUGGESTIONS FOR IMPROVING ORAL COMMUNICATION

Only a very few persons are gifted speakers naturally. Others have to practise hard to master this art of communication. Those aspiring to be good speakers must practise and learn the basics of body language. They should speak before mirrors, watch videos of good speakers studying their body language. They should deliver speeches before their friends for practice and make consistent efforts to master this art of expression through body language. Language is learnt through imitation. The same applies to body language but this imitation should be of some perfectionist and the practitioners of the art of communication. One should choose one's role-model judiciously and carefully.

The importance of body language and how to improve it have been discussed later in this book.

## QUESTIONS FOR DISCUSSION

1. Describe the qualities of good communication.
2. Describe the importance of body language in oral communication.
3. Suggest some important steps for the improvement of oral communication.

UNIT 3

# Skills of Communication

# 7

# Barriers to Communication

**LEARNING OBJECTIVES**

- To learn the various kinds of barriers that impede the smooth flow of communication.
- To learn how can barriers to communication be overcome.

## BARRIERS TO COMMUNICATION

Communication is successful when it is understood by the receiver. The receiver must get the meaning of the message as exactly as the sender wants to convey it. From our own experience we know that communication can never be hundred per cent complete. So many factors are involved in the process of communication and something can always go wrong. There may be so many reasons for the failure of communication or mis-communication. Mis-communication does not imply disagreement. It is called lack of communication. The factors that cause failure of communication are referred to as "barriers to communication".

### Noise

In the linguistic parlance 'noise' is referred to as interference or interruption. Often an oral communication is impeded through interruption. If two persons are interacting, a third person comes and interrupts the conversation; it is a barrier to communication. If there is a telephone call which impedes communication the listener may forget what has already been spoken to him. This kind of barrier to communication is known as "noise" and this is the commonest barrier to communication as it happens quite often.

### Code

To ensure effective communication the addresser and the addressee must share the same language. If the addressee speaks French and the addresser speaks English this language barrier will affect the process of communication. Even if they share the same language the level of difference in the competence in the use of language of the sender and the receiver may affect the smooth process of communication and may act as barrier to communication. In the case of oral communication the accentual patterns of the sender and the receiver may differ and may create barrier to communication.

### Vocabulary

If the sender uses subject-specific vocabulary it may not be understood by the receiver. If the speaker is a scientist and the listener knows nothing about science the terminology used by the sender will not be understood by the receiver. This will act as a barrier to communication

### Background

To make the communication effective and successful the sender and the receiver must share common background and assumptions. Lack of common background may make the comprehension of the message difficult and act as a barrier to communication.

### Cultural Differences

If the sender and the receiver do not share common culture the use of culture-specific vocabulary may impede the smooth process of communication and may act as barrier to communication.

### Environmental Disturbances

Environmental disturbances can impede communication. Even physical distance between the sender and the receiver can harm the process of communication.

### The Emotional States

Effective communication may be affected by the emotional states of the sender and the receiver. Mental state like anxiety, fear, lack of mutual trust, and rivalry may become barrier to communication.

In addition to general barriers to communication discussed above there are some sender specific and receiver-specific barriers, i.e., lapses on the part of the sender and lapses on the part of the receiver which act as barriers to communication.

## BARRIERS ON THE PART OF THE SENDER AND HOW TO OVERCOME THEM

1. If the message is not properly planned before its delivery the transmission of the message will not be smooth and it will lack clarity, precision and accuracy. The sender of the message should plan his message ahead. He/she should be very clear in his/her mind about the contents of the message and choose the right channel or medium of communication.
2. Sometimes the sender assumes that the receiver will understand what has already been conveyed. He/she assumes that the receiver is supposed to know the background and context of the matter. Depending on these assumptions he/she leaves gaps in the communication. These assumptions can become a barrier to communication. To overcome this barrier while planning the message the sender should try to understand the receiver's background and his/her

knowledge of the subject. He/she should use the familiar terms and try to anticipate the problems likely to be faced by the receiver in understanding and interpreting the message.

3. An English word has many different meanings. It is possible that the same word may convey two different meanings to two different persons. If the sender and the receiver assign different meanings to the word the message may be misunderstood. In such cases it will be helpful if the sender chooses his/her words carefully keeping in mind the problems that the receiver is likely to face. He/she may explain the meaning of technical and unconventional words. He/she may even restate the main points to ensure that the message has been correctly received.
4. If the sender lacks command over language and is unable to use appropriate and exact words the message will not be correctly understood by the receiver. The sender is expected to have complete command over language and he/she must choose his/her words very carefully. In the case of oral communication there should be no inconsistencies between verbal and non-verbal language. Facial expressions, gestures and postures should be according to the verbal language.
5. In professional dealings feelings like hatred, indifference, jealousy and prejudice have no place. While communicating the message the sender should take care that his/her personal liking or disliking or moods do not affect the smooth run of the communication.

## BARRIERS ON THE PART OF THE RECEIVER

1. The communication may not be received or understood correctly because of some lapses at the receiver's end. In the case of oral communication there may be disturbance caused by the noise coming from a roaring

bike or from the music being played during a marriage procession.

Such barriers to communication can be avoided if the receiver of the communication receives the communication in a place least likely to be invaded by such noises.

2. If the listener does not have the professional attitude towards his/her job or the professional training he/she may become inattentive. He/she may not pay the requisite attention to the communication due to boredom or because the subject is not of his/her interest.

   This kind of behaviour/conduct comes in the category of unprofessionalism. A great leader/manager has to rise above all these factors and pay due attention to whatever is being communicated to him/her.

3. Some receivers suffer from weaknesses like rigid beliefs and non-flexible approach. They are not interested in new ideas. This is also a barrier to communication.

   The receiver of the communication must rise above all these weaknesses and show great maturity in receiving and welcoming new ideas and information.

4. Where there is prejudice against the sender, where the receiver mistrusts the sender the message is likely to get distorted.

   The receiver should have an open mind and a positive attitude. When the receiver shows such attitude of trust and goodwill the communication is successful.

## OTHER BARRIERS TO COMMUNICATION

The formal communication network of an organization plays an important role in making the communication successful and effective. If this network limits the flow of communication to any particular direction, i.e., downward, upward, horizontal, it affects the proper and smooth flow of communication.

The formal channel of communication of a company must be efficient and error-proof. This will eliminate any chance of barrier to communication.

Some organizations adopt deceptive tactics by hiding the relevant information wholly or partially. This is a negative approach and amounts to barrier to communication. It is in the overall interest of the company to see that the communication flows freely. It should be honest and frank. Such an attitude pays in the long run.

The ability to plan well, the ability to choose and decide what to say and what not to say is a great virtue of the sender. It helps in the smooth flow of communication.

Since effective communication plays an important role in the successful conduct of an organization it becomes incumbent on both the sender and the receiver to make the communication efficient by eliminating all barriers to communication.

## OVERCOMING BARRIERS TO COMMUNICATION

The following steps can help to overcome the barriers to communication:

1. The sender must plan his message keeping in mind the cultural, social, geographical and educational background of the receiver.
2. The sender of the message should create an atmosphere of friendliness and mutual trust through the use of polite language and kind gestures.
3. The sender must give consideration to 'what to convey', 'where to convey' and 'when to convey'.
4. In case of face-to-face interaction the addresser should reinforce his/her words with action.
5. The message to be communicated must be clear. Simplicity of language will ensure clarity of the message. The sender should use only denotative words. Connotations suggest some extra meanings and may create confusion in the mind of the receiver.

## QUESTIONS FOR DISCUSSION

1. What do you understand by "barriers to communication?" Explain some of these.
2. How can barriers to communication be overcome?
3. What are the barriers to communication as far the sender is concerned? How can these barriers to communication be eliminated?
4. What are the barriers on the part of the receiver? How can these be overcome?

# 8

# Professional Communication

**LEARNING OBJECTIVES**

- To understand the meaning and importance of professional communication.
- To understand the meaning of the internal and external communication.
- To know the various kinds of letters like official letters, memos.

## IMPORTANCE OF PROFESSIONAL COMMUNICATION

In recent years the importance of professional communication has increased manifold. This is because of growing complexity in organizational behaviour. There has been rapid industrial growth and great advance in business management techniques. There is also the impact of modern technology on professional communication. Communication techniques have to meet the demands of fast changing business world. There is constant need for review and modification of professional communication system.

There is constantly growing realization by the professionals about the importance of professional communication. To meet the challenges of rapid industrial growth and globalization business houses are giving greater attention to professional communication techniques. The ability to communicate effectively has become key to the success of a business venture. No business organization can think of success without an efficient and competent system of communication at its disposal.

## THE ROLE OF PROFESSIONAL COMMUNICATION

It must be made clear here that professional communication is very different from personal communication. It is different in content, language, messages and even in the structure and form of writing. Personal communication is between friends and relatives and its aim is to promote friendship and goodwill. It may be about congratulating somebody on his success, expression of grief over some sorrowful event, exchange of greetings, or simply conveying massage.

Professional communication performs a number of functions for an organization. Its role in running and growth of the organization is significant. It has internal function as well as external function.

## INTERNAL FUNCTION IS USED TO:

As its internal function professional communication has to disseminate information within the organization. This communications is used:

1. direct and instruct the staff;
2. cultivate in the employees a feeling of belonging to the organization; and
3. motivate and encourage the employees and strengthen their morale.

Within the organization the employees are interested in the following kinds of information:

1. Information about advancement in career, pay and allowances and benefits like health insurance.
2. Overall objectives of the company, their role in the fulfilment of these objectives and how are they going to benefit from them.
3. Information about the working of other departments.
4. Working procedures and training facilities for advancement.

### *Important questions before the communication network*

The most important function of the internal system of communication is to decide–

1. What is the information that is to be conveyed?
2. Who requires this information?
3. The most suitable form of communication for the purpose.
4. The technique to be used for the dissemination of information.

## EXTERNAL FUNCTION

1. To exchange communication with other organizations, to exchange communication about buying and selling of goods and services.
2. To maintain liaison with other organizations.
3. To build goodwill of the company.

For the smooth flow of communication every organization maintains a network. This network decides who is to speak and to whom he has to speak and what to speak. Besides the formal channels of communication, there are also informal channels of communication. Sometimes the formal channels of communication do not prove effective. In such cases informal channels are used for communication.

Nowadays business organizations have many means of communication at their disposal. Some of the important means of communication are:

1. Electronic communication systems like computer, word processor, etc.
2. Teleprinter
3. Fax
4. Electronic mail
5. Voice mail
6. Telephone
7. Audio conference
8. Video conference
9. E-commerce

Most of the above mentioned means of communication have been discussed in detail later in this book.

In spite of the modern techniques of communication made available by technology, letter writing still remains the most important means of professional communication. Machines have taken over most of the common functions of an office. They have reduced the paper work considerably. Computers are being used for the storage of information and reproduction of documents. E-mails and video-conferences have brought a revolution in the techniques of communication. Yet the importance of letter writing as a means of professional communication has not waned.

Letter writing is an art. It is learnt and cultivated through practice. Its importance as means of professional communication hardly needs emphasis. Success of business organizations to a large extent, depends on the quality of letters sent. They can make or mar the reputation of a company. Therefore, companies pay great attention to professional communication through letters.

As an executive in a business organisation you have to write a number of letters everyday to persons you don't know personally. You have never seen them. Your letters reveal your personality, your attitude towards life and the standing of your company.

## PRINCIPLES OF LETTER WRITING

Letter writing involves thinking and planning. While writing letters take care of the following points:

1. Conceive the contents of the letter in your mind. When you have planned the contents of the letter, think how to begin the letter and how to conclude it. The matter must be well organized.
2. See that your letter contains only the relevant matter. Nothing superfluous should be there.
3. Politeness is the most important feature of a letter. It should reveal your positive outlook.
4. Language of the letter should be simple and easy to understand. Simplicity is a great virtue of a letter.

5. It should have no mistakes of spelling, grammar and punctuations, etc.

## IMPORTANCE OF PAPER AND LAYOUT

1. When somebody holds your letter in his hand the first thing he notices is the quality of the paper and instantly forms his opinion about the standing of your company. So the paper on which the letter is typed must be of a good quality.
2. The layout of the matter is also very important.
3. The letter should be well typed. There should be no mistakes of typing. There should be no overtyping or signs of the use of eraser or corrections.

## TYPES OF LETTERS

Normally the following types of letters has been used in offices:

1. Official letters
2. Memorandums
3. Circulars
4. Notices

Official letters are used for correspondence within the organization and for communication with other organizations. The structure of the official letters has already been discussed in Unit 5 chapter 2. The various subjects of business letters like letters of sales, credit, enquiries, orders, and claim have also been discussed in Unit 5.

## MEMO

The term memo is an abbreviation of the word memorandum. Like a letter it is a form of correspondence. Memos are briefly written communications for circulation within the organization. Memos are very useful means of sending information to a large number of people within the organization.

Memos are written in simple language. There is no scope for superfluous writing. They are written under pressure of time, so they are brief and to the point and are meant for wide circulation inviting instant response. They give the message in a straightforward manner.

## CIRCULARS/NOTICES

Circulars are letters meant for wide circulation. They are written in an objective manner. They are meant for dissemination of information to a large number of persons, may be to all the employees of a particular department or the organization. They are not addressed to any particular person or groups of persons. There are no salutations or complimentary closes. They circulate the information very briefly. A specimen of a circular/notice is given here.

**HERO AUTO INDUSTRIES LTD.**

**LUDHIANA**

2 March, 2012

**NOTICE**

The company has decided to grant interest-free loans to its employees for the purchase of cars. The selection of employees for the grant of loans will be made on the basis of the following criteria:

1. Length of service in the company,
2. Basic pay at the time of applying for loan,
3. Service record,
4. Distance of residence from the work place.

Interested persons may apply on the prescribed form to the undersigned by 15th March 2012.

**Manager**

Personnel Department

## QUESTIONS FOR DISCUSSION

1. Discuss the importance of effective communication for a business organization.
2. Discuss the role of internal communication network and external communication network.
3. Discuss the various means of professional communication.

# 9

# Interpersonal Communication and Methods to Improve It

## LEARNING OBJECTIVES

- To understand the meaning and importance of interpersonal communication.
- To learn how to improve interpersonal communication.

There are several levels at which communication takes place. These levels are:

1. Extrapersonal
2. Intrapersonal
3. Interpersonal
4. Organizational
5. Mass

## EXTRAPERSONAL

If communication takes place between a human being and a non-human being it is called extrapersonal. Non-human entities communicate through gestures, i.e., the movement of the various parts of the body. A dog moves its tail to express its gratitude to its master for some act of kindness.

## INTRAPERSONAL COMMUNICATION

Intrapersonal communication takes place within an individual. Every communication originates in the brain. It starts with the thinking process. This process may be called internal dialogue. Without this no further level of communication can take place.

## ORGANIZATIONAL LEVEL

Communication that takes place within an organization at different levels is called organizational communication. It is necessary for the smooth running of an organization.

## MASS COMMUNICATION

If the message is meant for a large audience it is sent through journals, books, advertisements, TV channels, newspapers, etc. It is impersonal in nature. Such a communication is called mass communication.

## INTERPERSONAL COMMUNICATION

Interpersonal communication means communication between persons and builds better relationship. Interpersonal skills of communication refer to mental abilities and communication skills which are applied during social conversation and interaction. These are used to achieve certain results. We can say that interpersonal skills are the abilities of an individual to get along well in an organization or within a social group. It also involves the ability to understand the perceptions, aspirations, etc., of human beings.

All living creatures communicate but only human beings use language as a medium of communication. It is through the medium of language that human beings build relationships. These relationships make them feel safe, secure and comfortable. As a social animal man cannot live alone. He needs the society of human beings to survive. He can feel happy and comfortable only when he has good relationship with his fellow human beings. His biological, social and materialistic needs compel him to seek the company of other human beings. He feels happy and easy in the company of fellow human beings. The primary need of human beings is to build and maintain relationships and build bridges of mutual trust and understanding. The main objective of interpersonal communication is to help people build better relationships.

## INTERPERSONAL COMMUNICATION DIFFERS FROM OTHER FORMS OF COMMUNICATION

The major differences are:

1. Only a few persons are involved in interpersonal communication. The interaction is limited to four or five persons.
2. In this kind of interpersonal communication participants are in close proximity to each other.
3. There are many sensory channels at service.
4. Immediate feedback is available

### Advantages of Interpersonal Communication

1. Since immediate feedback is available, doubts, if any, can be removed and clarifications can be sought.
2. In the case of inter-personal communication participants interact face to face. So non-verbal forms of communication can play an important role in the correct interpretation of the message.

## FORMAL OR INFORMAL

Interpersonal communication can be held at formal or informal level. If you go to the reception office of an airline to buy a ticket your communication is formal. But if you are having a casual talk with a friend or a family member your interpersonal communication is informal.

## VARIETY OF FACTORS

The situation in which interpersonal communication takes place guide the course of communication. These situations are:

1. The psychology of the participants.
2. The relationship between the participants.

3. The surrounding environment.
4. The cultural context.

## STEPS FOR THE IMPROVEMENT OF INTERPERSONAL COMMUNICATION

Ability to listen effectively is directly related to success in interpersonal skills of communication. Listening skills play an important role in our social, personal and professional life. At the place of work listening skills can minimize tensions and can help build better relationships. In personal life if we are willing to listen patiently the other's point of view many misunderstandings can be removed. During an interview the ability to listen effectively pays a lot.

Listening skill is very important as the first step to language learning. Language is learnt through imitation. A child is a great learner. It starts listening as soon as it is born and goes on listening whatever is spoken around it. This is how he takes the first step towards learning a language. Now we have at our disposal a number of channels for listening good English. We have radios, TV channels, record players and many other devices for listening good English. The most important factor that ensures perfection in the skills of interpersonal communication is competence in the art of listening and comprehension.

## HEARING AND LISTENING

Listening is the ability to understand and respond effectively to oral communication. There is difference between listening and hearing. Hearing does not need any conscious effort. Listening requires conscious effort on the part of the listener. Hearing is a physical process. Listening is a mental process. Hearing involves receiving sound signals. Listening requires the use of ears, brain and eyes. Listening is a more complex process and effective listening requires insights like perception. One can listen only when one makes a conscious effort. Hearing requires no effort. You hear the sounds made around you whether you want to hear or not.

## PROCESSES INVOLVED IN LISTENING

1. **Receiving:** The first process involved in listening is "receiving." Receiving means hearing the message physically and taking note of it. The listening process can be blocked by noise, impaired hearing or inattention of the listener.
2. **Interpreting:** Interpretation involves assigning meaning to sounds. It means understanding the message exactly as the speaker wants it to be understood.
3. **Storing the message:** The message needs to be stored for future references. It is called "remembering the message". One may take note of what one hears or make a mental outline of the message received.
4. **Evaluation of the message:** The receiver of the message evaluates the message by applying critical thinking skills. This is called evaluation of the message.
5. **Responding:** After evaluating the message the receiver of the message responds to the message through his/her reactions.

## BARRIERS TO LISTENING

Every sender of the message wishes that his/her communication should be understood and interpreted exactly as he/she wants it to be. His/her words should convey exactly the same meaning as he/she intends. But often this does not happen and messages are misunderstood or wrongly interpreted leading to great embarrassment. This is because of the various barriers to listening in operation. Some of the barriers to listening are discussed here.

## DISTRACTION

Often the process of listening is distracted. Distraction may be external or internal. It can be physical or mental. The noise made by the fans, glaring lights or loud music may cause distraction in the mind of the listener and the process of listening may suffer.

## LACK OF MOTIVATION

If the receiver of the communication lacks motivation, betrays inertia during conversation, lacks the will to face challenges, the process of listening will not be smooth. Smooth listening process requires motivation of the receiver.

## PERSONALITY TRAITS OF THE LISTENER

Success of the listening process also depends on the personality traits of the receiver. Persons who have very high opinion of themselves often fail to give due regard to the sender and take him/her lightly.

## PREJUDICE

If the receiver is not open-minded with a positive outlook, if he is prejudiced, the process of communication will suffer. The ability of the sender to send messages efficiently depends on the response of the receiver. Politeness and seriousness of purpose are infectious and they spread from the receiver to the sender.

## LOSS OF CONCENTRATION

Sometimes the receiver loses concentration especially if the conversation is long and full of complexities. In such cases the process of listening is hampered.

The success of the listening process depends directly on the ability of the sender in sending the message efficiently. If his/her message is not clear, if it lacks clarity, if the message lacks coherence and contains a lot of irrelevant matter, it will affect the performance of the listener and the message will not be received clearly. The sender should be very careful in planning and drafting his/her message.

## SPEAKING

Speaking is the second step to language learning. Success of interpersonal communication depends as much on the ability of the speaker to communicate well as on the ability of the receiver to receive the message accurately. If the message is not conveyed properly the process of interpersonal communication fails.

No language can be mastered without practice. As one cannot learn horse riding without sitting on the back of a horse, no one can master spoken language without a lot of practice.

The learning of phonetics, especially the phonetic transcription, is essential for the ability to pronounce the words correctly. The pronunciation of English words is arbitrary as there is no relationship between spellings and pronunciation. Moreover, English is a rhythm based language and therefore the knowledge and practice of stress system and accentual patterns is absolutely essential to communicate well in English.

## READING AND WRITING

The next step to language learning is reading. No one can master the various aspects of a language without reading literature.

Reading of fiction means learning a language through the art of dramatic narration. Practice in writing brings exactness in the writing of communication. Through practice in writing one learns to plan, write and communicate exactly what one wants to communicate.

In addition to perfection in the use of language one needs to have some more qualities of head and heart for competence in interpersonal communication.

These are –

1. **Ability to communicate well:** Ability to communicate well paves the way for good interpersonal skill.
2. **Affability:** Affability is a great virtue in interpersonal communication. It means the quality of being cheerful and friendly during the talk. What one can win through a happy smile cannot be won by any other method.
3. **Positive attitude:** During interpersonal communication one must focus on the positive side of the case and not on the negative side.

## APPRECIATIVE ATTITUDE

Some people look at the brighter side of the picture and appreciate profusely what deserves to be appreciated. One should avoid condemning, criticising or complaining. One should never talk ill of others.

## SENSE OF HUMOR

Some people are gifted with a sense of humour. Through this sense of humour they brighten the gloomy atmosphere.

## BODY LANGUAGE

The body language should radiate energy, enthusiasm and confidence.

## FRANKNESS AND TRANSPARENCY

Frankness, honesty and sincerity give you an image of a person who can always be trusted.

People like to talk to such persons and take interest in the communication.

## QUESTIONS FOR DISCUSSION

1. Discuss the various levels at which human communication takes place.
2. Discuss the meaning and importance of interpersonal communication. How does it differ from other forms of communication?
3. Discuss the steps for improving interpersonal communication.

UNIT 4

# Grammar

# 10

# Subject-verb Agreement (Concord)

## LEARNING OBJECTIVES

- To learn that in a sentence the form of the verb must agree with the subject in number and person.
- To learn to identify the real subject and know whether it is singular or plural.

Concord means agreement of the verb with the subject both in person and number. The verb must agree with the subject both in number and person.

**1. PERSON** – A subject can be of three persons such as:

(i) First person (I, we)

(ii) Second person (you)

(iii) Third person (he, she, it, they). There can be phrases like "my uncle", "your son". They are treated as third person subjects.

We use form of the verb according to the person of the subject.

### *Examples*

(i) I have a pen in my hand.

(ii) She has a pen in her hand.

(iii) They have pens in their hands.

### Examples

(i) I teach English.
(ii) You teach English.
(iii) She teaches English.

**2.** In the Present Indefinite Tense a third person singular subject takes a verb inflected with 's' or 'es'.

### Examples

(i) I teach in a college.
(ii) You teach in a college.
(iii) She teaches in a college.
(iv) They teach in a college.

*Similarly*

(i) I do not like smoking.
(ii) You do not like smoking.
(iii) She does not like smoking.
(iv) They do not like smoking.
(v) Do I teach English?
(vi) Does she teach English?
(vii) Do they teach English?

**3. Number:** A subject may be singular or plural. A singular subject takes a singular verb. A plural subject takes a plural verb.

### Examples

(i) He goes to school.
(ii) They go to school.

**4. Use of have/has:** We use 'have' with first person pronouns "I" and "We", with second person pronoun "you" and with third person plural pronouns as "They". We use 'has' with a third person singular subject.

### *Examples*

(i) I have had my meal.
(ii) We have enjoyed our share of luck.
(iii) You have got admission in BITS.
(iv) They have obtained permission.

*But*

(i) He has done it again.
(ii) She has stopped coming.

## The Important Rules of Concord

The most important thing is the identification of the subject and find out whether it is singular or plural.

**Rule 1:** If two singular nouns are joined with "and" the subject becomes plural and takes a plural verb.

### *Examples*

(i) Mohan goes to school.
(ii) Sohan goes to school

*But*

1. Mohan and Sohan go to school.
2. Two and two make four.
3. Sita and Sheela are sisters.
4. Rita and Deepika go to the village well to fetch water.

## Exceptions to this Rule

1. If two singular nouns joined by "and" refer to one unit, the subject remains singular and the verb is singular.

### *Examples*

(i) The horse and the cart is at the door.
(ii) Bread and butter is his only food.

2. If two singular nouns joined by "and" refer to one idea, the subject is singular and it takes a singular verb.

***Example***

(i) Slow and steady wins the race.

3. If two singular nouns are joined with "and" and they refer to distance or weight, the verb is singular.

***Examples***

(i) 500 km is a long distance.
(ii) 100 kg is a great weight.

**Rule II.** If two singular nouns are joined with either ... or, neither, nor the subject is singular and the verb is singular.

***Examples***

(i) Mohan or Sohan has to do it.
(ii) Sheela or Ragini opens the door.
(iii) Either Ram or Shyam paints the door.
(iv) Neither he nor his brother is to blame.
(v) Neither Sarla nor her daughter sings well.

**Rule III.** If a singular noun and a plural noun are joined with either/or, neither/nor, the subject is plural and the plural word is placed near the subject.

***Examples***

(i) Either Mohan or his sons plough the land.
(ii) I or my sons are to blame.
(iii) Either the Principal or the teachers supervise the parade.
(iv) Neither the captain nor the players lodge a protest during the match.
(v) Neither Deepika nor her daughters are intelligent.

**Rule IV.** If a singular word is joined with singular or plural words with the help of words/phrases like 'with', 'together with', 'along with', 'as well as' – the subject is singular and it takes a singular verb.

***Examples***

(i) The Principal, with all the staff members, has gone to Jaipur.
(ii) The old man, together with his children, lives in that hut.
(iii) The woman, along with his daughters, goes to work in a factory.
(iv) The Director, as well as all the faculty members, work very hard.

**Rule V. Subject with "one of".** The phrase "one of" is always followed by a plural noun. But the subject is singular and it takes a singular verb.

***Examples***

(i) One of the boys is absent.
(ii) One of our servants cheats every one.
(iii) One of the teachers lives in my neighborhood.

*but*

If a relative clause follows expressions such as "one of the best" , "the first of many" and the like and when the relative clause refers to the class as a whole and not to one member of the class, the verb is plural.

***Example***

This is one of the richest gold mines that have been discovered.

**Rule VI.** The case of each, every one

1. Each and every one are singular words. They take singular verbs.

### *Examples*

(i) Each boy signs well.
(ii) Every one lives happily here.

2. When each, either, everyone are followed by plural words the subject remains singular and the verb is singular.

### *Examples*

(i) Each one of the boys is responsible.
(ii) Every one of the women is trying to win.
(iii) Each one of the members enjoys working there.
(iv) Every one of the teachers works honestly.

**Rule VII.** Nearness of the verb with the subject.

Nearness of the verb with the subject often misleads us. We have to identify the real subject.

### *Examples*

(i) The students of this Institute are sincere.
(In the above case the real subject is 'students' although this institute is placed near the verb).
(ii) This institute with about 1000 students enjoys a unique reputation.
In the above sentence the real subject is 'institute' although the plural noun 'students' is placed near the verb.
(iii) This Institute which has more than 1000 students gives the best education.
In the above written sentence the real subject is 'this institute' although "students" is placed near the verb.

### The Case of Collective Nouns

Collective nouns like committee, council, government, police, army can be treated as singular or plural subjects depending on their use.

***Examples***

(i) The committee is unanimous on this point (the use of committee does not show any division. So it is singular

*but*

The committee were divided on this issue. (In this sentence it is clear that committee has more than one member. It is plural.

**The Subject Following the Verb**

Normally the subject precedes the verb. The structure of the sentence in such cases is:

"subject + verb + object."

But sometimes the subject follows the verb and the structure of the sentence becomes " object + verb + subject" . In such cases the writer must make sure that the verb agrees with the subject

*Wrong.* Before the country lies great problems of rising prices, unemployment and social security.

*Right.* Before the country lie great problems of rising prices, unemployment and social security.

***None.*** After none, used as a subject, the verb is plural if "none" refers to a number of units.

Verb is singular if it refers to a word expressing mass, in which case the idea of separate units is not present.

***Examples***

(i) None of the members were present.
(ii) None of the sugar was spilled,

Some writers always use a singular verb after 'none' . This is the older practice and is still correct but it is being supplanted by the one given above.

### 'Verb' after introductory 'there'

After the introductory word 'there', the verb is singular if the subject – which follows the verb – is singular; verb is plural if the subject is plural.

***Examples***

(i) There is one objection to the plan.
(ii) There are several objections to the plan.

### Nouns Plural in form but Singular in Meaning

Some nouns, which are plural in form but singular in meaning, take singular verbs.

***Examples***

(i) Mathematics is an interesting subject.
(ii) The United States is a great country.

## EXERCISES

1. Correct the following sentences:
   (i) Neither the size nor the colour of the gloves were right.
   (ii) 100 km are not a long distance.
   (iii) The beating of the drums were heard far off in the jungle.
   (iv) Two and two makes four.
   (v) Either Mohan or Sohan are to blame.
   (vi) His shirt, as well as his overcoat, were found near the police station.
   (vii) Bread and butter are his favourite food.
   (viii) Every one of them are waiting outside.
   (ix) The captain, as well as his team mates, have lined up for the national anthem.
   (x) Have either of these recommendations been accepted by the Chairman.

2. Correct the following sentences:
   (i) The first two chapters of this book was written by Vivekanand.
   (ii) The Principal, together will all the staff members, have left for Jaipur.
   (iii) From this institute has come out not only great writers but also great teachers.
   (iv) The Prime Minister, with the members of his Cabinet, are required to attend the meeting.
   (v) One of the students are absent.
   (vi) Neither of us have had dinner, so we shall stop for it in the next town.
   (vii) Each one of the boys were shouting.
   (viii) Only the income from these funds are to be used for current expenses.
   (ix) The prisoner, together with his guards, were taken to the court.
   (x) Everyone in the audience were cheering widely.

3. Correct the following sentences:
   (i) From each city has come reports about the communal violence.
   (ii) Every man, woman, and child are invited to be present.
   (iii) There has been great many changes in the syllabus this year.
   (iv) The committee is requested to invite their friends.
   (v) The jury are in session.
   (vi) Before us to the south lies the Kashmir valley and the Rose Garden.
   (vii) On this marble memorial is engraved the names of some brave soldiers who sacrificed their lives for the country.
   (viii) The cheapness of the article, together with its durability, make it very desirable.
   (ix) Why is there so many errors in your composition?
   (x) Mary's sisters is absent.

4. Supply the correct forms of the verbs:
   (i) Here __________ the Principal and the Vice Principal (come, comes)
   (ii) _____ there four or five rooms in this cottage? (is, are)
   (iii) Every one of these articles _______ been written to promote love and peace. (has, have)
   (iv) Neither the landlady nor the tenant _____ present at the time of burglary. (was, were)
   (v) Lying on the table ___________ a book and a duster. (was,were)
   (vi) None of the members ______ present (was, were)
   (vii) Slow and steady _________ the race. (win, wins)
   (viii) Either Raj or Dev _______ to play the part of the hero. (is, are)
   (ix) One of his memorable stories _______ published in the Times magazine. (was, were)
   (x) Each of the ten men _________ been asked to report at the headquarters. (has, have)

5. Supply the suitable forms of verbs in the blanks provided below:
   (i) Neither the Principal nor the staff members _________ present in the meeting. (was, were)
   (ii) The secretary-cum accountant ______ conducting the proceedings. (is, are)
   (iii) Everybody ______ entitled to have the right to speak. (is, are)
   (iv) Mohan, along with his wife, ________ looking into the matter. (is, are)
   (v) A few students _______ able to get admission in M.A. classes. (was, were)
   (vi) Neither of the proposals made by me ________ accepted by the committee. (was, were)
   (vii) Bread and butter ______ the only food he likes. (is, are)
   (viii) Quite a number of students of this class _____ found absent. (was, were)

(ix) My wife, together with our children, _____ gone on a pilgrimage. (has, have)

(x) The committee _________ looking into the matter. (is, are)

6. Correct the following sentences:
   (i) Both Ram and Sita has gone to the forest.
   (ii) Either Mohan or Sohan are to blame.
   (iii) The plays of Shakespeare is very popular.
   (iv) The poems of Milton has high seriousness.
   (v) The students of BKBIET is known for their discipline.
   (vi) The most interesting thing about these plays are that they teach moral values.
   (vii) The long and the short of his advice are that one should conduct oneself in a dignified manner.
   (viii) A report of the meeting, as well as a list of new officers, are presented on the fourth page.
   (ix) Each of the witnesses were summoned to appear in court on Monday
   (x) He is one of the boys that plays the violin in the band.

7. In each of the following sentences supply a verb in agreement with its subject:
   (i) The news ________ true (is, are)
   (ii) Rustom and Sohrab ________ Persiasn heroes. (was, were)
   (iii) Neither Mohan nor his friends ______ present (is, are)
   (iv) Three Musketeers _______ an interesting novel. (is, are)
   (v) There __________ 20 students in this class. (is, are)
   (vi) A packet of sweets ______ given to each child (was, were)
   (vii) He, with his father, _____ the first to arrive (was, were)

(viii) The cost of all these articles ________ risen (have, has)

(ix) Where ______ all the students gone? (have, has)

(x) Forty yards _____ a good distance.

## ANSWERS

**1.**

(i) Neither the colour nor the size of the gloves was right.

(ii) 100 km is not a long distance.

(iii) The beating of the drum was heard far off in the jungle.

(iv) Two and two make four.

(v) Either Mohan or Sohan is to blame.

(vi) His shirt, as well as his coat, was found near the police station.

(vii) Bread and butter is his favourite food.

(viii) Every one of them is waiting outside.

(ix) The captain, as well as his team mates, has lined up for the national anthem.

(x) Has either of these recommendations been accepted by the Chairman?

**2.**

(i) The first two chapters of this book were written by Vivekanand.

(ii) The Principal, together with all the staff members, has left for Jaipur.

(iii) From this institute have come out not only great writers but also great teachers.

(iv) The Prime Minister, with the members of his Cabinet, is requested to attend the meeting.

(v) One of the students is absent.

(vi) Neither of us has had dinner, so we shall stop for it in the next town.

(vii) Each one of the boys was shouting.

(viii) Only the income from these funds is to be used for current expenses.

(ix) The prisoner, together with his guards, was taken to the court.

(x) Everyone in the audience was cheeringly wildly.

**3.**

(i) From each city have come reports about the communal violence.

(ii) Every man, woman, and child is invited to be present.

(iii) There have been great many changes in the syllabus this year.

(iv) The committee are requested to invite their friends.

(v) The jury is in session.

(vi) Before us to the south lie the Kashmir valley and the Rose Garden.

(vii) On this marble memorial are engraved the names of some brave soldiers who sacrificed their lives for the country.

(viii) The cheapness of the article, together with its durability, makes it very desirable.

(ix) Why are there so many errors in your composition.

(x) Mary's sisters are absent.

**4.**

| | | | |
|---|---|---|---|
| (i) come | (ii) are | (iii) has been | (iv) was |
| (v) were | (vi) was | (vii) wins | |
| (viii) is | (ix) was | (x) has | |

**5.**

| | | | | |
|---|---|---|---|---|
| (i) were | (ii) is | (iii) is | (iv) is | (v) were |
| (vi) was | (vii) is | (viii) | were | (ix) has |
| (x) is | | | | |

**6.**

(i) Both Ram and Sita have gone to the forest.

(ii) Either Mohan or Sohan is to blame.

(iii) The plays of Shakespeare are very popular.

(iv) The poems of Milton have high seriousness.

(v) The students of BKBIET are known for their discipline.

(vi) The most interesting thing about these plays is that they teach moral values.

(vii) The long and short of his advice is that one should conduct oneself in a dignified manner.

(viii) A report of the meeting, as well as a list of new officers, is presented on the fourth page.

(ix) Each of the witnesses was summoned to appear in court on Monday.

(x) He is one of the boys that play violin in the band.

**7.**

| | | | | |
|---|---|---|---|---|
| (i) is | (ii) were | (iii) are | (iv) is | (v) are |
| (vi) was | (vii) was | (viii) has | (ix) have | (x) is. |

# 11

# Linking Words (Conjunctions)

**LEARNING OBJECTIVES**

- ➢ To understand the use of coordinating conjunctions (connectives) like "and, but, yet, still, although, though, however, etc."
- ➢ To learn the use of relative pronouns like who, which, what, why, as connectives forming compound and complex sentences.

A 'linking word' is a word that joins words, phrases or sentences, for example, and, but, or, yet, so, therefore, etc., are linking words.

Linking words are also called conjunctions or connectives.

A conjunction may have one word like "and, "but", etc. It may have more than one word like "as well as", "not only but also", etc.

Linking words are also used for transforming simple sentences into compound sentences and complex sentences.

### What is a simple sentence?

A simple sentence is made up of only one clause (it has one subject, one verb and one object (adverb is optional).

### *Example*

Tendulkar plays cricket.

### Complex Sentence

A complex sentence is made of one independent clause and one or more dependent clauses.

### *Example*

I know that he is a thief.

### Compound Sentence

A compound sentence is made of two or more independent clauses.

### *Example*

He is a teacher but his wife is a doctor.

### Coordinating Conjunctions

Words such as 'and' but that connect clauses or sentences of equal importance (independent clauses) are called coordinating conjunctions.

### List of Coordinating Conjunctions

The following is the list of coordinating conjunctions.

And, as well as, not only, but also, but, still, yet, however, nevertheless, or else, otherwise, either, or, neither nor, therefore, for, so.

### Uses of Coordinating Conjunctions

(i) And

We use "and" for joining clauses of the same nature.

***Example***

*Simple sentences*

(i) Rekha is very beautiful
(ii) She works in films.

**Compound sentence:** Rekha is very beautiful and she works in films.

### Use of "as well as"

We use "as well as" for joining things of the same nature (like/and).

***Example***

*Simple sentences*

(i) English is an important subject.
(ii) Computer Science is an important subject.

**Compound sentence:** English, as well as Computer Science, is an important subject.

### Use of "not only but also"

We use "not only but also" in place of 'and' but this phrase states the facts more emphatically.

***Example***

*Simple sentences*

(i) Shakespeare is a great poet.
(ii) He is a great dramatist.

**Compound sentence:** Shakespeare is not only a great poet but he is also a great dramatist.

### Use of "but"

We use 'but' to join two clauses contrasting in meaning.

***Example***

*Simple sentences*

(i) Ram is rich.
(ii) He is miser.

**Compound sentence:** Ram is rich but he is miser.

**Use of still/yet**

Still and yet are used in the sense of "but" but the contrast is less sharp. Still and yet are used more in the sense of "in spite of".

***Example***

*Simple sentences*

(i) He worked hard.
(ii) He failed.

**Compound sentence:** He worked hard, yet he failed.

**Use of However, Nevertheless**

"However" and "nevertheless" are used in the sense of "in spite of".

***Example***

*Simple sentences*

(i) He does not deserve.
(ii) I shall help him.

**Compound sentence:** He does not deserve, however I shall help him.

**Use of "or", "else", "otherwise"**

We use "or", "else" and "otherwise" to make a choice between two things.

### *Example*

*Simple sentences*

(i) My son will come.
(ii) If not, he will inform me.

**Compound sentence:** My son will come or (else, otherwise) he will inform me.

### Use of "Either or"

We use "either or" to make a choice between two options.

### *Example*

*Simple sentences*

(i) Ram is to blame.
(ii) Shyam is to blame.

**Compound sentence:** Either Ram or Shyam is to blame.

### Use of "neither" or "nor"

We use 'neither, nor' to make a choice between two negative options.

### *Example*

*Simple sentences*

(i) He did not break the glass.
(ii) His wife did not break the glass.

**Compound sentence:** Neither he nor his wife broke the glass.

### Use of "Therefore", "and", "so"

"Therefore" and "so" are the conjunctions of result.

***Example***

*Simple sentences*

(i) Dravid was suffering from fever.
(ii) He could not play.

**Compound sentence:** Dravid was suffering from fever, so (therefore) he could not play.

### Use of Relative Pronouns, Interrogative pronouns as conjunctions

Relative pronouns like who, whose, which, what are also used as connectives. Interrogative pronouns are also used as connectives.

### Use of whose

We use 'whose' for persons and things.

***Example***

*Simple sentences*

(i) The woman has gone mad.
(ii) Her husband was killed.

**Compound sentence:** The woman whose husband was killed has gone mad.

### Which

Which is used as a relative pronoun in place of that

***Example***

*Simple sentences*

(i) He has finished the work.
(ii) He began it yesterday.

**Compound sentence:** He has finished the work which he began yesterday.

**What**

'What' is used for things. It is used as a pronoun.

***Example***

I say what I mean.

**Where (place)**

***Example***

She did not tell where she lived.

**How: (as a conjunction of reason)**

***Example***

We do not know how the thieves entered the house.

**Whether/If**

The conjunctions of 'whether' or 'if' are used to state a condition.

***Example***

We don't know whether (if) he will come.

**Although**

The conjunction of 'although' is used in place of "in spite of".

***Example***

Although he is ill, he will come.

**Since, as, because**

We use the conjunctions of 'since' 'as' and 'because' to state the reason.

***Example***

Since (as, because) he is ill, he will not come.

Relative pronouns like who, whom, that, which, whose are also used as connectives (linking words to join two clauses).

### Defining Relative Clauses

Defining relative clauses define or identity which person or thing is being referred to. The pronouns used are who, whom, that and which. There is no comma before a defining relative clause.

### Non-defining Relative Clauses

It gives extra information about somebody or something. Thus extra information is seperated from the main clause by a comma. Pronoun used are who, whom, which and whose.

## EXERCISES

I. Supply the missing conjunctions in the following sentences:

(i) Tendulkar is a batsman ______ he bats at number 5

(ii) My father, _________, my aunt is coming to see me.

(iii) Raj Kapoor was _________ a great actor _______ also a great director.

(iv) Gopal is poor ________ he is honest.

(v) He attempted only three questions, ________ he passed.

(vi) Alok is not a regular employee, __________ he works hard.

(vii) My son will come by rail ________ he will come by air.

(viii) _________ Dravid _________Sehwag will lead the team.

(ix) ____________ the Principal ___________ the Vice Principal attended the meeting.

(x) He has not secured 55 per cent marks, ______ he cannot appear in NET.

(xi) The man, ______ pocket was picked, is here.

II. Add the missing conjunctions in the following sentences:

(i) I have read the book _________ you gave me yesterday.

(ii) I don't know ________ he fared in the examination.

(iii) _______ he applies for the job, he will be selected.

(iv) We don't know ________ he will come or not.

(v) We are politically free ________ we are not free economically.

(vi) She is both lazy _______ dull.

(vii) The place _______ she works is near my house.

(viii) My boss was highly pleased with _____ I did.

(ix) We both love _________ honour our Director.

(x) She is very rich _______ she is miser.

III. Supply the missing conjunctions in the following sentences:

(i) ________ he is intelligent, he does not make a show of it.

(ii) I do not know ________ he will come or not.

(iii) Although he was injured, ______ he continued running.

(iv) Shyam is rich ______ his brother is poor.

(v) He is your friend _______ you should help him.

(vi) She is very beautiful _______ she likes to wear beautiful clothes.

(vii) He is not rich _______ he likes to live a luxurious life.

(viii) He did not work hard _______ he managed to get through the examination.

(ix) I say _______ I mean.

(x) Do you know ________the Director lives.

IV. Join the following sets of sentences to make one sentence of each set?

1. (i) He is an adventurous man.
   (ii) He loves climbing mountains.
2. (i) He passed the written examination of I.A.S.
   (ii) He could not clear the interview.
3. (i) She is quite pretty.
   (ii) She is ill mannered.
4. (i) I was ill.
   (ii) I could not attend the interview.
5. (i) He did not do well.
   (ii) He was promoted.
6. (i) I do not know.
   (ii) When she will respond to my communication.
7. (i) They are not on good terms.
   (ii) They help each other.
8. (i) Tendulkar was injured.
   (ii) He could not play.
9. (i) Munshi Prem Chand was a patriot.
   (ii) He was a great writer.
10. (i) Behave yourself.
    (ii) I will teach you a lesson.

## SOLUTIONS

**I.**

(i) and (ii) as well as (iii) not only, but also
(iv) but (v) yet (vi) yet
(vii) or (viii) either, or (ix) neither nor
(x) so (ix) whose.

**II.**

(i) that or which (ii) how (iii) if
(iv) whether (v) but (vi) and
(vii) where (viii) what (ix) and
(x) but

**III.**

(i) though/although (ii) whether (iii) yet

(iv) but (v) and (vi) and (vii) still (yet)
(viii) yet (ix) what (x) where

**IV.**

(i) He is an adventurous man and loves climbing mountains.
(ii) He passed the written examination of I.A.S. but could not clear the interview.
(iii) She is quite pretty but she is ill mannered.
(iv) I was ill, so (therefore) I could not attend the interview.
(v) He did not do well, yet he was promoted.
(vi) I do not know when she will respond to my communication?
(vii) They are not on good terms, yet they help each other.
(viii) Tendulkar was injured, so (therefore) he could not play.
(ix) Munshi Prem Chand was not only a patriot but he was also a great scholar.
(x) Behave yourself or I will teach you a lesson.

# 12

# Relative Clauses

## LEARNING OBJECTIVES

- ➢ To know the meaning of relative clauses and their importance in written communication.
- ➢ To know the difference between defining and non-defining relative clauses.

## WHAT IS A CLAUSE?

A clause is a group of words that includes a subject and a verb. It forms a part of a sentence. It is a small sentence within a sentence.

### *Examples*

1. A sentence of one clause
   "She is an engineer".

   A sentence of two clauses
   She is an engineer and she works in a government office.

The above sentence has the following two clauses:

(i) She is an engineer.
(ii) She works in a government office.

2. The man, who came late, is the boss.
   The above sentence has the following two clauses:
   (i) The man came late.
   (ii) He is the boss.

3. He earns, she spends and they enjoy.
   The above sentence has the following three clauses:
   (i) He earns.
   (ii) She spends.
   (iii) They enjoy.

Clauses within a sentence are joined by linking words, also called coordinators and subordinators like "and, as well as, but, yet, so, still, who, which, that, whose, etc."

## RELATIVE CLAUSES

Relative clauses are parts of compound/complex sentences. These clauses are joined with the help of coordinators and subordinators.

Complex sentences are made with the help of relative pronouns like whom, that, which, whose.

### *Examples*

(i) The man, who is compering the show, is a great actor.
(ii) Mary, whom no body had seen before, arrived late.
(iii) He is sitting at the desk that faces the window.
(iv) The books, which I have borrowed from the library, are very interesting.
(v) Mary, whose husband had died last month, is still in grief.

Compound sentences are made with the help of coordinators like and, but, yet, still, so, as well as, and with the help of relative pronouns like who, which, whose, etc.

### *Examples*

(i) She is poor but she is honest.

(ii) Ram, together with his brother, is going to the forest.

## DEFINING RELATIVE CLAUSES

Defining relative clauses define or identify which person or thing you are talking about.

### *Example*

The man who lives in our neighbourhood is the Manager.

There is no comma before a defining relative clause. The pronouns used in the defining relative clauses are who, whom, that, which. We call them relative pronouns.

## USE OF RELATIVE PRONOUNS

### The use of "who" or "that"

We use 'who' or 'that' when the subject is a person.

### *Examples*

(i) The girl who approached me is my cousin

or

The girl that approached me is my cousin.

### Use of "that" or "which"

We use the pronoun "that" or "which" when the subject is a thing.

### *Examples*

I am reading the book that I borrowed from the library.

or

I am reading the book which I borrowed from the library.

### Use of "who", "that" "whom"

We use "who", "that" and "whom" when the object is a person (the relative pronoun may be omitted).

***Examples***

She is the girl who/that/whom I met last night.

or

She is the girl I met last night.

or

She is the girl whom I met last night.

**We use "which", when the object is a thing (Relative pronouns can be omitted).**

***Examples***

I have completed the work that was given to me.

or

I have finished the book you lent me.

or

I have typed the letter which you asked me to type.

or

I have typed the letter you asked me to type.

**Use of "whose"**

We use 'whose' to show that something belongs to somebody.

***Example***

The government granted a lot of money to the woman whose house had been burnt.

**NON-DEFINING RELATIVE CLAUSES**

Non-defining relative clauses give extra information about somebody or something. If this additional information is left out from the sentence the sentence would still be complete and make sense. This extra information is always enclosed within commas to separate it from the main clause.

***Example***

"My wife, who lives in Chandigarh, is very beautiful."

We can leave out the extra information : 'Who lives in Chandigarh'. The sentence then would be "My wife is very beautiful". This is a complete sentence and it makes sense.

The following pronouns can be used in non-defining clauses:

Who, whom, which and whose.

**The use of "who"**

We use "who" when the subject is a person.

***Example***

My friend, who is the Principal of a college, is coming to see me.

**Use of "which"**

We use "which" when the subject is a thing.

***Example***

The books, which have recently arrived in the library, are very useful.

**Use of "who" or "whom"**

We use "who" or "whom" when the subject is a person.

***Example***

Mohan, who nobody had seen before, arrived late.

or

Mohan, whom nobody had seen before, arrived late.

### Use of "which"

We use "which" when the subject is a thing.

The tickets, which have been paid for, are still valid.

### Use of "whose"

We use "whose" when something belongs to somebody.

***Example***

Sheela, whose house was damaged, has applied for compensation.

## NOMINATIVE, OBJECTIVE AND POSSESSIVE FORMS OF RELATIVE PRONOUNS

Relative pronouns have the following three forms:

(i) *Nominative case:* It refers to the subject of the sentence.

***Example***

The book which I sent you is by Wordsworth.

(ii) *Objective case:* The relative clause refers to the object of the sentence.

***Example***

That is the pen which I lost.

(iii) *Possessive case:* The relative pronoun "whose" is used when something belongs to somebody.

***Example***

Sheela, whose article was published in the Time magazines, lives in the U.S.A.

Relative pronoun "which" has the same form for the singular and plural cases.

***Examples***

(i) The book which I sent you is costly.
(ii) The books which I sent you are costly.

The relative pronoun "which" has no possessive case. But we use "whose" as a substitute for "of which".

***Example***

The tree whose leaves are green gives good shadow.

***Use of "that"***

The relative pronoun "that" is used both in the nominative case and the objective case.

***Examples***

(i) He that is well satisfied is well paid (nominative case).
(ii) Take anything that you like (objective case).

It means the relative pronoun "that" has the same form for the nominative and objective cases. It has also the same form in the singular and plural sentences.

**Use of "what"**

The relative pronoun "what" is used in the singular. It has the same form with nominative and objective cases.

***Examples***

I mean what I say. You can take what you like.

Her father promised to gift her whatever she desired.

## USE OF RELATIVE ADVERBS AS LINKING VERBS

They describe time, place, reason and manner of activity.

(i) Do you know when he will come back?
(ii) Do you know where the President of India lives?
(iii) I do not know how you can survive on such a meagre salary?
(iv) Can you guess why he misbehaved with me yesterday?

## USE OF INTERROGATIVE PRONOUNS

(i) Can you tell me who is waiting at the door?

(ii) I do not know whom she wanted to meet.
(iii) I wonder whose car is parked there.
(iv) We do not know what he wants.
(v) He asked her which bike was hers.

## USE OF RELATIVE PRONOUNS AS LINKING WORDS

Words like "who", "whom", "which", "that", "which" (relative pronouns) are also used as linking words.

### *Examples*

(i) This is the man who committed bank robbery.
(ii) The lady whom we met the other day was our teacher.
(iii) This is the girl whose grandfather died yesterday.
(iv) The scooter that you purchased is of the best quality.
(v) The car which is parked there is mine.

## USE OF COMPOUND RELATIVE PRONOUNS AS LINKING WORDS

(i) Whosoever wants to join us may raise his land.
(ii) Whoever gets ninety per cent or more marks will be granted a scholarship.
(iii) You will get whichever you want.

## EXERCISES

1. Fill in the blanks with suitable relative pronouns.
   (i) This is the student ________ is on top of the class.
   (ii) This is the man _____ son has won the game.
   (iii) The film ______ was shot in Rajasthan is ready for release.
   (iv) This is the actor _____ we like.
   (v) These are the parents _______ children are here.

(vi) Those are the keys ______ I lost.

(vii) He ________ is content is happy.

(viii) I know ___________ she likes.

(ix) The man _______ is brave speaks the truth.

(x) He prayed best ______loved best.

2. Fill in the blanks with suitable relative pronouns.

(i) The fort _____ you saw was built by Pandavs.

(ii) The flowers ________ grow in this garden are very beautiful.

(iii) He _____ does his best shall never fail.

(iv) God helps those _____ help themselves.

(v) I did not know that Miss Dipika _____ I met yesterday was your sister.

(vi) The book _______ you gave me is very enjoyable.

(vii) Where is the book _____ I gave you?

(viii) I do not believe ______ you say.

(ix) The man __ has not seen Lahore has seen nothing.

(x) Is this the road _____ leads to Agra ?

3. Fill in the blanks with suitable relative pronouns.

(i) His wife is a woman ______ likes to dress well.

(ii) Did the hat ______ you were wearing yesterday really belonged to you?

(iii) The article ______ you wrote is very interesting.

(iv) The leader, ______ many people had never heard before, addressed a gathering last night.

(v) The skylark, ______ sings very sweet songs, builds its nest on the ground.

(vi) You should not miss the movie "Gladiators" ______ is the finest action move.

(vii) The Taj Express, ________ should arrive at 2:30 is on time.

(viii) The University of Rajasthan, ________ is one of the oldest universities is known for its excellence.

(ix) Pride, _______ is an evil, brings destruction.

(x) Shakespeare, _________ is the world's greatest dramatist, was born in a small village.

4. Add relative pronouns to the following:

(i) The lady, ______ had been married for only a month, lost her husband in an accident.

(ii) What is the name of the man ______ wife was caught stealing?

(iii) The old gentleman _______ lives in my neighborhood has eight children from his first wife.

(iv) It is a wise child _________ knows his father.

(v) People _________ live in glass houses should not throw stones at others.

(vi) The man _____ is selling bangles is my brother-in-law.

(vii) The food ____ we had for lunch was well-cooked.

(viii) Hockey, _______ is a good sport, makes us strong.

(ix) Can you tell me _______ is happening there?

(x) Name the player _______ has scored 100 centuries in first class cricket.

5. Add relative pronouns in the following sentences:
   - (i) Can you name the bowler _____ has taken the maximum number of wickets in test cricket?
   - (ii) Do you know the name of the country _______ he belongs to?
   - (iii) Can you tell the colour of the shirt ______ he was wearing?
   - (iv) A large number of persons _____ had gone to see the match could not get tickets.
   - (v) We do not know in ______ car Kapil Dev had driven to the ground.
   - (vi) The man _______ pocket has been picked, is the President of CCI.
   - (vii) I should like to see the shop ______ sells old books.
   - (viii) Do you know ______ he wanted for his birthday present?
   - (ix) He killed the woman ______ he loved and worshipped.
   - (x) I can't say _______ is going to happen tomorrow.

6. Join together each of the following pairs of sentences using relative pronouns:
   - (i) The students clapped heartily. They were watching the match.
   - (ii) Mohan indulged in indiscipline. He was punished.
   - (iii) Gold is found in West Indies. It is a precious metal.
   - (iv) The girl plays good tennis. You see her there.
   - (v) The woman is ill. I saw her yesterday.

(vi) I heard the news. It astonished me.

(vii) The thief stole the watch. He has been caught.

(viii) We can see the dog. It bit the girl.

(ix) The man is brave. He is respected

(x) He is a scoundrel. No one trusts him.

7. Combine the following pairs of sentences by means of non-defining relative pronouns:

(i) Julius Ceaser conquered England twice. He was a Roman General.

(ii) Charles Dickens visited America twice. He was a great English writer.

(iii) The great fire of London destroyed a large part of the city. It broke out in 1666.

(iv) John Milton became blind when he was in mid-fifties. His poem "Paradise Lost" is a classic.

(v) Jane Austen knew everything about love and marriage. She never got married.

(vi) Emily Dickinson died young. We love her poetry very much.

(vii) New Delhi attracts many tourists. It is the capital of India.

(viii) A dog is considered to be the most faithful creature. It is a four legged animal.

(ix) My wife lives in Chandigarh. She is very beautiful.

(x) The World War I destroyed many beautiful places. It started in 1914.

8. Combine the following ideas by means of defining or non-defining relative clauses:

(i) I am sure it was Ram. He told Shiela to do it.

(ii) What was the name of the soldier? He came here last night?

(iii) The matter has been settled. You were arguing about it last night.

(iv) The ship was beautiful. It has been sunk.

(v) He was reading the book. It was given to him by the principal.

(vi) He was living with his step mother. She was not kind to him.

(vii) The Prime Minister visits the poor people living in huts. He lives in a mansion.

(viii) Thomas Gray was a voracious reader. He wrote beautiful poetry.

(ix) Ernest Hemingway was a great fiction writer. His novel "The Old Man and the Sea" won him Nobel Prize for literature.

(x) Lord Ram was a great king. He spent fourteen years in the forest.

(xi) Meena Kumari was a gentle lady. She was a great actress.

## ANSWERS

1.

(i) who (ii) whose (iii) which

(iv) whom (v) whose (vi) which

(vii) who (viii) whom (ix) who

(x) who

2.

(i) which (ii) which (iii) who

(iv) who (v) whom/that (vi) which/that
(vii) which/that (viii) what (ix) who
(x) which/that

3.

(i) who (ii) which (iii) which/that
(iv) whom (v) that (vi) which
(vii) which (viii) which (ix) which
(x) who

4.

(i) who (ii) whose (iii) who
(iv) who (v) who (vi) who
(vii) which/that (viii) which (ix) what
(x) who

5.

(i) who (ii) which/that (iii) which/that
(iv) who (v) which (vi) whose
(vii) which/that (viii) what (ix) whom
(x) what

6.

(i) The students, who were watching the match, clapped heartily.

(ii) Mohan, who indulged in indiscipline, was punished.

(iii) Gold, which is a precious metal, is found in West Indies.

(iv) The girl, whom you see there, plays good tennis.

(v) The woman, whom I saw yesterday, is ill.

(vi) The news, which I heard, astonished me.

(vii) The thief, who stole the watch, has been caught.

(viii) We can see the dog which bit the girl.

(ix) The man, who is brave, is respected.

(x) He is a scoundrel whom no one trusts.

7.

(i) Julius Creaser, who was a Roman General, conquered England twice.

(ii) Charles Dickens, who was a great English writer, visited America twice.

(iii) The great fire of London, which broke out in 1666, destroyed a large part of the city.

(iv) John Milton, whose poem "Paradise Lost" is a classic, became blind in his mid-fifties.

(v) Jane Austen, who never got married, knew everything about love and marriage.

(vi) Emily Dickinson, whose poetry we love very much, died young.

(vii) New Delhi, which is the capital of India, attracts many tourists.

(viii) A dog, which is a four-legged animal, is considered to be the most faithful creature.

(ix) My wife, who lives in Chandigarh, is very beautiful.

(x) The World War, which started in 1914, destroyed many beautiful places.

8.

(i) I am sure it was Ram who told Shiela to do it.

(ii) What was the name of the soldier who came here last night?

(iii) The matter, which you were arguing about last night, has been settled.

(iv) The ship, which has been sunk, was very beautiful.

(v) He was reading the book which was given to him by the Principal.

(vi) His grandmother, with whom he was living, was not kind to him.

(vii) The Prime Minister, who lives in a mansion, visits the poor people living in huts.

(viii) Thomas Gray, who wrote beautiful poetry, was a voracious reader.

(ix) Ernest Hemingway, whose novel "The Old Man and the Sea" won him Nobel Prize for literature, was a great fiction writer.

(x) Lord Ram, who spent fourteen years in the forest, was a great king.

(xi) Meena Kumari, who was a great actress, was a gentle lady.

# 13

# Common Errors

## LEARNING OBJECTIVES

- To know the kinds of grammatical errors usually committed in written English.
- To learn how to write grammatically correct English.

## ERRORS IN THE USE OF TENSES

| Wrong | Right |
|---|---|
| (i) He is going to school everyday. | He goes to school everyday. |
| (ii) She has received a letter of appointment yesterday. | She received a letter of appointment yesterday. |

### Use of Present Tense

#### *Difference between the present indefinite tense and present continuous tense*

Present indefinite (simple) tense is used for habitual actions and general truths, not necessarily now. Present continuous tense is the real present. It describes what is happening now (at present). Present simple tense is used to refer to some permanent situation. Present continuous tense is used for some temporary situation.

In the present simple tense we use the plain verb. It is inflected with 's' or 'es' when the subject of the sentence is third person singular. In the case of a negative sentence the inflection of 's' or 'es' is transferred to the helping verb (auxiliary) do. Adverbs used with present indefinite tense are: 'daily, every day, every week, every month , usually, generally, rarely, seldom, often etc.

Adverbs used with the present continuous tense are – "now", "at present"

| | **Wrong** | **Right** |
|---|---|---|
| i | Mangoes are tasting sweet. | Mangoes taste sweet. |
| ii | We now learn French. | We are now learning French. |
| iii | The man who walk past the window is living next door. | The man who is walking past the window lives next door. |
| iv | The sun shines brightly now. | The sun is shining brightly now. |
| v | The sky is getting dark in the evening. | The sky gets dark in the evening. |
| vi | The baby cries because it is hungry now. | The baby is crying because it is hungry now. |
| vii | Does he often goes to see movies? | Does he often go to see movies? |
| viii | I sit on a chair and eating an apple now. | I am sitting on a chair and eating an apple now. |
| ix | The sun is rising in the east. | The sun rises in the east. |
| x | Does she loves dancing? | Does she love dancing? |
| xi | When your wife cooks food? | When does your wife cook food? |

| | | |
|---|---|---|
| xii | I like mangoes but she like apples. | I like mangoes but she likes apples. |
| xiii | I do not play cricket, he do not play hockey. | I do not play cricket, he does not play hockey. |
| xiv | Is it raining in summer? | Does it rain in summer? |
| xv | Mohan likes dancing but his sons likes singing. | Mohan likes dancing but his sons like singing. |
| xvi | Fish swims in water. | Fish swim in water. |
| xvii | Do you know where Mohan live? | Do you know where Mohan lives? |
| xviii | Take an umbrella. It rains now. | Take an umbrella. It is raining now. |
| xix | Students do not always behaves nicely. | Students do not always behave nicely. |
| xx | He has fallen into the river. I try to get him out. | He has fallen into the river. I am trying to get him out. |
| xxi | Australian sheep gives good milk. | Australian sheep give good milk. |
| xxii | Prices rise slowly and gradually now. | Prices are rising slowly and gradually now. |
| xxiii | A storm comes, keep indoors. | A storm is coming. Keep indoors. |

## USE OF MODALS IN THE PRESENT INDEFINITE TENSE

Plain verbs in the present indefinite tense are not inflected with 's' or 'es' when they come after modals.

| | Wrong | Right |
|---|---|---|
| i | She knows English well and can answers all your questions. | She knows English well and can answer all your questions. |

| | | |
|---|---|---|
| ii | If he wants he may appears in the examination. | If he wants he may appear in the examination. |
| iii | Must he leaves before the supper or should he stays a little longer. | Must he leave before the supper or should he stay a little longer? |
| iv | He plays tennis well but he cannot plays cricket. | He plays tennis well but he cannot play cricket. |
| v | If your son is tired he ought to spends a holiday by sea. | If your son is tired he ought to spend a holiday by sea. |
| vi | He thinks his wife may comes later. | He thinks his wife may come later. |
| vii | Can he finds the money he has lost? | Can he find the money he has lost? |
| viii | He needn't bothers about small problems. | He needn't bother about small problems. |
| ix | They go to Kashmir every year but it may seems impossible this year. | They go to Kashmir every year but it may seem impossible this year. |
| x | May she goes out? | May she go out? |

## VERBS NOT USED IN THE CONTINUOUS TENSE

The following verbs are usually not found in the continuous tense. If they are used in the continuous tense they convey a different shade of meaning, e.g., Taste believe, feel, know, think, see, hear, notice, recognize, smell.

### *Example*

(i) I see your point (not – I am seeing your point)

but

You are seeing hallucinations these days.

| | Wrong | Right |
|---|---|---|
| i | I am hearing you are getting married soon. | I hear you are getting married soon. |
| ii | I am seeing you are wearing your best clothes. | I see you are wearing your best clothes. |
| iii | I am smelling something burning in the kitchen. | I smell something burning in the kitchen. |
| iv | I am remembering your name now. | I remember your name now. |
| v | I am believing he is telling a lie. | I believe he is telling a lie. |
| vi | I am hoping he is doing well. | I hope he is doing well. |
| vii | Milk is tasting sweet. | Milk tastes sweet. |
| viii | I am feeling I am suffering from fever. | I feel I am suffering from fever. |
| ix | I am refusing to admit that he is cheating me. | I refuse to admit that he is cheating me. |
| x | It is appearing that he is understanding the problem now. | It appears that he understands the problem now. |

## PRESENT PERFECT TENSE AND PAST INDEFINITE TENSE

The present perfect tense should not be used to refer to an actively that took place at some definite point of time in the past. When we have to refer to some activity that took place at some definite point of time in the past we use past indefinite tense. The present perfect tense expresses the completion or 'perfection' of an action by now.

| | Wrong | Right |
|---|---|---|
| i | He has left a minute ago. | He left a minute ago. |
| ii | She has come to see me yesterday. | She came to see me yesterday. |
| iii | When have you got the news of his promotion? | When did you get the news of his promotion? |
| iv | Until a year ago, the business of the company has been flourishing. | Until a year ago, the business of the company was flourishing. |
| v | He has stopped working after the death of his wife. | He stopped working after the death of his wife. |
| vi | Mohan has received a letter of congratulation last Sunday. | Mohan received a letter of congratulation last Sunday. |
| vii | She has not gone to the beauty parlour last night. | She did not go to the beauty parlour last night. |
| viii | Can you believe that she has rung me four times / Since we quarrelled. | Can you believe that she rang me four times / Since we quarrelled. |
| ix | She has quarrelled with her husband twice after the dinner. | She quarrelled with her husband twice after dinner. |
| x | She has not topped the list of successful candidates last year. | She did not top the list of successful candidates last year. |

## PRESENT CONTINUOUS SIMPLE AND PRESENT PERFECT CONTINUOUS

Present continuous tense is used to relate an action that is continuing at the time of speaking. It has no relation with the past. Present perfect continuous tense is used to relate an action that started at some definite point of time in the past and it is continuing in the present.

Adverbials in the present continuous tense, now, at present.

### Present Perfect Continuous Tense

Adverbs used in the present perfect continuous tense.'Since' for point of time like 'since Monday', 'since 15th June', 'since January'. We use 'for' to refer to period of time 'for four days', 'for' a month' etc.

#### *Examples*

| | Wrong | Right |
|---|---|---|
| i | He is working since morning. | He has been working since morning. |
| ii | Are you reading for an hour now? | Have you been reading for an hour now? |
| iii | I am waiting here for two hours but she has not come. | I have been waiting here for two hours but she has not come. |
| iv | He is reading in the same class for three years. | He has been reading in the same class for three years. |
| v | She has been learning English now. | She is learning English now. |
| vi | He is climbing the mountain since morning but has not yet reached the top. | He has been climbing the mountain since morning but has not yet reached the top. |
| vii | The officer is ringing the bell for five minutes but the peon has not turned up. | The officer has been ringing the bell for five minutes but the peon has not turned up. |

| | | |
|---|---|---|
| viii | What are you doing since morning? | What have you been doing since morning? |
| ix | Are you waiting long for me? | Have you been waiting long for me? |
| x | What were you doing since I have been out? | What have you been doing since I have been out? |

## ERRORS IN THE USE OF PAST INDEFINITE AND PAST PERFECT TENSES

### Use of Past Indefinite Tense and Past Perfect Tense

Two actions take place. Both these actions take place in the past. But these actions do not take place at the same time. One action takes place earlier than the other. The action which takes place earlier is also known as pre-past. This tense is called past perfect. For the action which takes place later we use the past indefinite tense.

**Verbs: Past Perfect Tense – had+past participle**

***Past Indefinite : past***

| | Wrong | Right |
|---|---|---|
| i | She thanked me for what I did. | She thanked me for what I had done. |
| ii | I was sorry that I hurt him. | I was sorry that I had hurt him. |
| iii | Why didn't you post the letter after I told you to do? | Why didn't you post the letter after I had told you to do? |
| iv | In France he soon forgot what he learnt earlier. | In France he soon forgot what he had learnt earlier. |
| v | The girl asked what happened to her ice cream? | The girl asked what had happened to her ice cream? |

| | | |
|---|---|---|
| vi | My wife ate all the food before I reached home. | My wife had eaten all the food before I reached home. |
| vii | The patient died before the doctor came. | The patient had died before the doctor came. |
| viii | The thieves ran away before the police arrived | The thieves had run away before the police arrived. |
| ix | When I had reached the station, the train left. | When I reached the station, the train had left. |
| x | He told me how the accident took place. | He told me how the accident had taken place. |

## ERRORS IN THE USE OF CONDITIONAL SENTENCES

### Use of Tense Forms in the Conditional Sentences

| Nature of the condition | Tense in the conditional clause | Tense in the main clause |
|---|---|---|
| **Open** (a condition that is likely to be fulfilled in future). | **Present indefinite**<br>If I go to Jaipur | **Future indefinite**<br>I shall bring your books |
| **Rejected condition** (a condition that was not fulfilled in the past, so the result was not achieved. | **Past perfect**<br>If I had known, | Future perfect (use of "would", "should", "might")<br><br>I would have phoned you |
| **Imaginary Unreal** | **Past indefinite**<br>"Became" or "were"<br>If I were you,<br><br>If I became the P.M., | Use of "would"<br>I would not do this.<br>I would remove poverty. |

| | Wrong | Right |
|---|---|---|
| i | If I shall go to Jaipur, I shall bring books for you. | If I go to Jaipur, I shall bring books for you. |
| ii | You will spoil the things if you will not be careful. | You will spoil the things if you are not careful. |
| iii | If it rained, I shall play at home. | If it rains, I shall play at home. |
| iv | He would have failed if he did not work hard. | He would have failed if he had not worked hard. |
| v | If you had shown patience, you will have won the match. | If you had shown patience, you would have won the match. |
| vi | I shall join my duty on 5th September if I shall receive the appointment letter before this date. | I shall join my duty on 5th September if I receive the appointment letter before this date. |
| vii | Had I reached there in time, I shall have saved his life. | Had I reached there in time, I would have saved his life. |
| viii | If I were in your place, I shall not do this. | If I were in your place, I would not do this. |
| ix | He will have run over a child if he had not stopped his car. | He would have run over a child if he had not stopped his car. |
| x | I may remove poverty if I became the Prime Minister. | I would remove poverty if I became the Prime Minister. |

## AGREEMENT OF THE VERB WITH THE SUBJECT (CONCORD)

The verb must agree with the subject both in number and person. A singular subject takes a singular verb and a plural subject takes a plural verb.

## Some Rules of Concord

(i) If two singular nouns are joined with "and" the subject becomes plural and takes a plural verb. But if two singular nouns joined with the help of "and" point to one unit, one idea or they refer to distance or weight the subject is singular and it takes a singular verb.

(ii) If two singular nouns are joined with "either", or "neither", nor the subject is singular and it takes a singular verb.

(iii) If a singular noun and plural noun are joined with "either", or "neither", "nor" the subject is plural and the plural word is placed near the subject.

(iv) If a singular subject is joined with plural words with the help of words like "with", "together with", "along with", "as well as" the subject is singular.

(v) Some nouns which are plural in form but singular in meaning take a singular verb (Example: News, Mathematics)

(vi) A collective noun takes a singular verb when the collective noun is thought of as a whole, a plural verb when individuals of which it is composed are thought of.

(vii) When the subject follows the verb instead of preceding it, the verb should agree with the subject

(viii) When there are words intervening between the subject and the verb, the verb should agree not with the nearest noun but with the real subject.

| | **Wrong** | **Right** |
|---|---|---|
| i | Either Ram or Sita are to blame. | Either Ram or Sita is to blame. |
| ii | On the desk lies his book and pencil. | On the desk lie his book and pencil. |

| | | |
|---|---|---|
| iii | Neither of them have returned. | Neither of them has returned. |
| iv | The *Arabian Nights* have delighted many children. | The *Arabian Nights* has delighted many children. |
| v | Mohan with his friends were punished. | Many with his friends, was Mohan punished. |
| vi | A packet of sweets were given to each child. | A packet of sweets was given to each child. |
| vii | The quality of these mangoes are good. | The quality of these mangoes is good. |
| viii | Neither the size nor the colour of the gloves were right. | Neither the size nor the colour of the gloves was right. |
| ix | In this book is recorded the name and address of every student. | In this book are recorded the name and address of every student. |
| x | This is one of the most inspiring poems that has ever been written. | This is one of the most inspiring poems that have ever been written. |
| xi | Why is there so many people on the road? | Why are there so many people on the road? |
| xii | The students of this institution is exceptionally intelligent. | The students of this institution are exceptionally intelligent. |
| xiii | Bread and butter are his only food. | Bread and butter is his only food. |
| xiv | One of the boys were hurt. | One of the boys was hurt. |
| xv | None of the stolen articles have been recovered. | None of the stolen articles has been recovered. |
| xvi | It is one of the most interesting plays that has been produced in Bombay. | It is one of the most interesting plays that have been produced in Bombay. |

| | | |
|---|---|---|
| xvii | Only the income from these funds are used for the current expenses. | Only the income from these funds is used for the current expenses. |
| xviii | The Prime Minister, with the members of his Cabinet, are to be present at the ceremony. | The Prime Minister, with the members of his Cabinet, is to be present at the ceremony. |
| xix | From this institution has come not only many great scholars but also great entrepreneurs. | From this institution have come not only many great scholars but also great entrepreneurs. |

## SEQUENCE OF TENSES

The sequence of tenses should indicate the logical time relation between the parts.

| | **Wrong** | **Right** |
|---|---|---|
| i | He bought the house so that he may have a home in his old age. | He bought the house so that he might have a home in his old age. |
| ii | They said they will be here next week. | They said they would be here next week. |
| iii | If he cannot come, he would let you know. | If he cannot come, he will let you know. |
| iv | He said that the earth moved round the sun. | He said that the earth moves round the sun. |
| v | He says he would join the N.C.C. camp the next month. | He says he will join the N.C.C. camp the next month. |
| vi | Move only when you were asked to do so. | Move only when you are asked to do so. |
| vii | The work was easy as the factory is equipped with proper machinery. | The work was easy as the factory was equipped with proper machinery. |

| | | |
|---|---|---|
| viii | He said that he is leaving for London the next day. | He said that he was leaving for London the next day. |
| ix | She said that she is living in Paris. | She said that she was living in Paris. |
| x | They always stayed at the same expensive hotel, for they have plenty of money. | They always stayed at the same expensive hotel, for they had plenty of money. |

## ERRORS IN THE USE OF DETERMINERS

### The use of Indefinite Article a/an

We use "a" before consonant sounds. We use "an" before vowel sounds.

(i) Use a/an before a singular countable noun when it is being used for the first time.

(ii) Use a/an before professions.

(iii) Use a/an in phrases like at a loss, to be in a temper, at a glance, etc.

(iv) Use a/an before some illnesses like 'to have a cold' to have a sore throat.

| | **Wrong** | **Right** |
|---|---|---|
| i | He is lecturer but his wife is engineer. | He is a lecturer, but his wife is an engineer. |
| ii | Please give me an glass of water. | Please give me a glass of water. |
| iii | He is a intelligent person and he works in an university. | He is an intelligent person and he works in a university. |
| iv | Dog is a lot more useful animal than cat. | A dog is a lot more useful animal that a cat. |
| v | I can go to movie today. | I can go to a movie today. |

| | | |
|---|---|---|
| vi | I have toothache. | I have a toothache. |
| vii | He is not Shakespeare. | He is not a Shakespeare. |
| viii | He has bought pair of trousers. | He has bought a pair of trousers. |
| ix | Little knowledge is a dangerous thing. | A little knowledge is a dangerous thing. |
| x | He is Indian, his wife is German. | He is an Indian, his wife is a German. |

## DEFINITE ARTICLE 'THE'

"The" is very much related to "this" and "that".

"The" specifies and identifies. There are three kinds of specifications:

(i) Anaphoric: It points backward to a person or thing – "I bought a pen", "The pen writes well".

(ii) Cataphoric: It points to a person or thing described by a phrase, for instance, "the book on the table".

**Homophoric:** The specification is in the situation.

Use "the"

(i) Before unique things like the sun, the moon, the universe, the earth, etc.

(ii) Before historical buildings like the Taj Mahal, the Red Fort etc.

(iii) Before the names of religious books "the Gita". "the Bible", "the Kuran"

(iv) Before the names of trains like the "Bikaner Mail", the "Taj Express"

(v) Before the names of newspapers, "The Hindu", "The Indian Express"

(vi) Before the names of rivers, canals, deserts, mountains (not before single peaks) like "The Ganges", "The Sahara Desert".

(vii) Before the name of a country only if the name suggests that it is made of some states, regions, etc. for instance "the U.S.A. and if the " name of a country is preceded by words like "Republic, Emirate etc.

(viii) If we use plural nouns, substances or meals in a general way (not specific) we do not put any article before them. But if we refer to some specific plural nouns, substances, or meals we use "the" before them.

(ix) Use article "the" before the superlative degrees of adjectives.

(x) No article is used before the names of languages and games.

| | **Wrong** | **Right** |
|---|---|---|
| i | Man who came to see me is an engineer. | The man who came to see me is an engineer. |
| ii | Sun always rises in the east. | The sun always rises in the east. |
| iii | Read first chapter. | Read the first chapter. |
| iv | Taj Mahal is a beautiful building. | The Taj Mahal is a beautiful building. |
| v | I always keep 'Gita" in my house. | I always keep 'The Gita' in my house. |
| vi | He is travelling by Bikaner Mail. | He is travelling by the Bikaner Mail. |
| vii | I read Indian Express. | I read the Indian Express. |
| viii | My son lives in U.S.A. and often goes to Russia. | My son lives in the U.S.A. and often goes to Russia. |

| | | |
|---|---|---|
| ix | Water in that pot is not fit for drinking. | The water in that pot is not fit for drinking. |
| x | The wheat is grown in Punjab and Haryana. | Wheat is grown in Punjab and Haryana. |
| xi | He told me that he was returning after having a holy dip in Ganges which flows from Himalayas. | He told me that he was returning after having a holy dip in the Ganges which flows from the Himalayas. |
| xii | He was one of holiest men. | He was one of the holiest men. |
| xiii | Many big ships sail over Atlantic Ocean. | Many big ships sail over the Atlantic Ocean. |
| xiv | Letter you sent me was received only yesterday. | The letter you sent me was received only yesterday. |
| xv | The elephants are used to pull heavy loads. | Elephants are used to pull heavy loads. |
| xvi | What are we having for dinner today? | What are we having for the dinner today? |
| xvii | There are five continents in universe. | There are five continents in the universe. |
| xviii | The wood floats on water but the iron does not. | Wood floats on water but iron does not. |
| xix | The English is a global language. | English is a global language. |
| xx | Tendulkar plays the cricket. | Tendulkar plays cricket. |

### "Some" and "Any"

We use 'some' and 'any' to refer to unspecified quantity. The simple rule for the use of 'some' and 'any' is, use some before positive statements and 'any' before negative statements and interrogative sentences.

| | Wrong | Right |
|---|---|---|
| i | He asked me for ice but I can't find some. | He asked me for ice but I can't fine any. |
| ii | There is some tea in the kitchen but there isn't some milk. | There is some tea in the kitchen but there isn't any milk. |
| iii | I can't eat some more apples but I should like any more oranges. | I can't eat any more apples but I should like some more oranges. |
| iv | Do you want some bananas? | Do want any bananas? |
| v | You can take these eggs if you want any more. | You can take these eggs if you want some more. |
| vi | I have lost my pencil. Have you some to lend me? | I have lost my pencil. Have you any to lend me? |
| vii | These apples are stale. Please give me any new ones. | These apples are stale. Please give me some new ones. |
| viii | She asked me for some money but I haven't some money in the bank. | She asked me for some money but I haven't any money in the bank. |
| ix | Have you some spare pillows. We haven't some with us. | Have you any spare pillows. We haven't any with us. |
| x | Ask her if she wants any more cakes, but we haven't any biscuits just now. | Ask her if she wants some more cakes, but we haven't any biscuits just now. |

## ERRORS IN THE USE OF PREPOSITIONS

1. "At" as a preposition of time

(i) We use "at" to express fixed timing (for a certain moment or a point of time). We use "at" before "noon" sunset, midnight. We also use "at" in expressions like at the end of the debate, at the beginning of the lesson.

(ii) We use "at" as a preposition of time for a period which marks a point in the year like "at Christmas".

2. "On" as a preposition of time

   (i) We use "on" before a specific or particular day of the festival like "on Diwali day".

   (ii) We use "on" before specific days either the name of the day or date or a special occasion.

**Important:** We do not use any preposition if there is an adjective (next, last) before the noun indicating day.

### Use of "in" as a Preposition of Time

(i) "In" is used before months and years.

(ii) Before "morning", "afternoon", "evening".

(iii) We use "in" also to show the total length of time taken for the completion of an activity.

### During as a Preposition of Time

We use "during" to express an idea that an activity continued throughout the specific period.

**"By"** is used to tell the latest time by which the work must be completed.

**"Since"** we use for point of time.

**"For"** for period of time.

## Prepositions of Place

(i) We use of "in" before places in a general way like "in the world" in the universe.

**(ii) Cities, towns, villages**

Normally we use "in" before "cities" and "at" before small towns or villages.

## Place of Residence

We use "in" before place of residence like "in a house, in a flat, in a quarter, in a bungalow". But if the place is given a specific name, we use "at" before it like "at Anand Bhawan", "at the White House".

## Place of Work

If the place of work is a building use "in" before it. For example "in a bank", "in a school", "in an office".

If the place of work is a building which has a name use "at" before it.

| | **Wrong** | **Right** |
|---|---|---|
| i | I shall go to Delhi on next Monday. | I shall go to Delhi next Monday. |
| ii | She came to see me on last Saturday. | She came to see me last Saturday. |
| iii | The town observed a complete strike Sunday last. | The town observed a complete strike on Sunday last. |
| iv | I hope to go to Bombay Saturday next. | I hope to go to Bombay on Saturday next. |
| v | We have a week's holiday on Christmas. | We have a week's holiday at Christmas. |
| vi | We light lamps at Diwali day. | We light lamps on Diwali day. |

| | | |
|---|---|---|
| vii | We have a holiday for the Republic Day. | We have a holiday on the Republic Day. |
| viii | We go for a walk during the evening. | We go for a walk in the evening. |
| ix | Most of the actors live at big bungalows. | Most of the actors live in big bungalows. |
| x | Poor people live at huts. | Poor people live in huts. |
| xi | Rajesh Khanna used to live in "Ashirwad". | Rajesh Khanna used to live at "Ashirwad" |
| xii | Nehrus lived in Anand Bhawan. | Nehrus lived at Anand Bhawan. |
| xiii | The house was burgled in the night. | The house was burgled during the night. |
| xiv | I woke up during midnight to receive a call. | I woke up at midnight to receive a call. |
| xv | Ambanis live on a big mansion. | Ambanis live in a big mansion. |
| xvi | My friend works in the Rail Bhawan. | My friend works at the Rail Bhawan. |
| xvii | In his childhood Shakespeare lived in Stratford on Avon. | In his childhood Shakespeare lived at Stratford-on-Avon. |
| xviii | He writes in pen. | He writes with a pen. |
| xix | Ram is trembling in fear. | Ram is trembling with fear. |
| xx | Heaven is not going to fall at your head. | Heaven is not going to fall on your head. |
| xxi | We have to compete with a strong team. | We have to compete against a strong team. |
| xxii | Mohan and Sohan can learn grammar with no teacher. | Mohan and Sohan can learn grammar without a teacher. |

| | | |
|---|---|---|
| xxiii | She has been suffering from fever for Monday. | She has been suffering from fever since Monday. |
| xxiv | Believe of God and do the right. | Believe in God and do the right. |
| xxv | Visitors are allowed during 3.00 p.m. and 4.00 p.m. | Visitors are allowed between 3.00 p.m. and 4.00 p.m. |
| xxvi | He lives on a rented flat. | He lives in a rented flat. |
| xxvii | My friend works in Town Hall. | My friend works at Town Hall. |
| xxviii | Sarita works on a school. | Sarita works in a school. |
| xxix | The boy jumped in the well. | The boy jumped into the well. |
| xxx | He was killed by a knife. | He was killed with a knife. |
| xxxi | He does not like to part of his money. | He does not like to part with his money. |
| xxxii | The audience heard him in patience. | The audience heard him with patience. |
| xxxiii | Will you come to see me on tomorrow? | Will you come to see me tomorrow? |
| xxxiv | We saw a movie on yesterday. | We saw a movie yesterday. |
| xxxv | Usually the shops are closed on every Sunday. | Usually the shops are closed every Sunday. |
| xxxvi | She comes to her village on every weekend. | She comes to her village every weekend. |
| xxxvii | Applications must be submitted upto 15th July. | Applications must be submitted by 15th July. |
| xxxviii | He is with love. | He is in love. |
| xxxix | She is into trouble. | She is in trouble. |
| xxxx | Come and see me during evening. | Come and see me in the evening. |

## ERRORS IN THE USE OF WORDS

| | Wrong | Right |
|---|---|---|
| i | I hope my request will be excepted. | I hope my request will be accepted. |
| ii | He exceeded to my request. | He acceded to my request. |
| iii | I hope I shall be able to adapt the new methods in my teaching. | I hope I shall be able to adopt the new methods in my teaching. |
| iv | The advise of parents is very useful. | The advice of parents is very useful. |
| v | He faced the averse circumstances bravely. | He faced the adverse circumstances bravely. |
| vi | The affect of his advice was good. | The effect of his advice was good. |
| vii | You should have no allusion about her admiration for you. | You should have no illusion about her admiration for you. |
| viii | He is already to take the examination. | He is all ready to take the examination. |
| ix | Love is not love if it altars when it alteration finds. | Love is not love if it alters when it alteration finds. |
| x | He has acsented to my request. | He has assented to my request. |
| xi | This scheme will be beneficient to the farmers. | This scheme will be beneficial to the farmers. |
| xii | His childish manners reveal a pure soul. | His childlike manners reveal a pure soul. |
| xiii | Pay my complements to your parents. | Pay my compliments to your parents. |

| | | |
|---|---|---|
| xiv | He has made considerate contribution to the success of his scheme. | He has made a considerable contribution to the success of the scheme. |
| xv | He has been speaking continually for an hour or so. | He has been speaking continuously for an hour or so. |
| xvi | What he says is hardly creditable. | What he says is hardly credible. |
| xvii | He was not able to complete the work because the machine was deficient. | He was not able to complete his work because the machine was defective. |
| xviii | Television is the greatest discovery of the modern world. | Television is the greatest invention of the modern world. |
| xix | The thief refused the charge. | The thief denied the charge. |
| xx | A man who has attained the age of 20 is illegible to vote. | A man who has attained the age of 20 is eligible to vote. |
| xxi | Prof. Krishna Mohan is an imminent scholar of English. | Prof. Krishna Mohan is an eminent scholar of English. |
| xxii | One should not be enviable of the success of others. | One should not be envious of the success of others. |
| xxiii | He is incited about the offer of a new job. | He is excited about the offer of a new job. |
| xxiv | The candidate was formally employed in a reputed organization. | The candidate was formerly employed in a reputed organization. |

| | | |
|---|---|---|
| xxv | Dr. Dool Singh worked as an Honourable Secretary for a number of years. | Dr. Dool Singh worked as an Honorary Secretary for a number of years. |
| xxvi | To help those in trouble is a human action. | To help those in trouble is a humane action. |
| xxvii | Gurgaon is an industrious town. | Gurgoan is an industrial town. |
| xxviii | Mohan has made a judicial choice of his career. | Mohan has made a judicious choice of his career. |
| xxix | If you are busy I can come and see you latter. | If you are busy I can come and see you later. |
| xxx | Please don't loose your patience. | Please don't lose your patience. |
| xxxi | The officious version of the accident is quite contrary to the version given by eyewitnesses. | The official version of the accident is quite contrary to the version given by eyewitnesses. |
| xxxii | Have they tried to overcome the practicable difficulties? | Have they tried to overcome the practical difficulties? |
| xxxiii | It is against my principals to help criminals. | It is against my principles to help criminals. |
| xxxiv | I shall precede further in the matter after I get instructions from you. | I shall proceed further in the matter after I get instructions from you. |
| xxxv | We should be respectable to our teachers. | We should be respectful to our teachers. |
| xxxvi | Man cannot live alone. He is a sociable animal. | Man cannot live alone. He is a social animal. |

| | | |
|---|---|---|
| xxxvii | Classrooms should be specious. | Classrooms should be spacious. |
| xxxviii | Government should provide stationery items free to students. | Governments should provide stationery items free to the students. |
| xxxix | Verbose messages have no records. | Verbal messages have no records. |
| xxxx | The country needs jealous workers to spread the message of communal harmony and peace. | The country needs zealous workers to spread the message of communal harmony and peace. |

UNIT 5

# Composition

14. Resume Writing
15. Business Letter Writing—Sales, Credit, enquiry, Order, Claim, Complaint, Job Applications, etc.
16. E-mail Messages
17. Telephone Etiquettes

# 14

# Resume Writing

**LEARNING OBJECTIVES**

- To provide practical guidance for preparing an attractive resume and also to show how letters accompanying the resume are wirtten.

Resume is a statement of facts which includes a summary of your educational and academic background. It includes research experience, work experience, etc. It also gives information about the awards and honours won. It should also highlight interests, hobbies, etc. In a nutshell a good resume should give all the information which makes you a suitable candidate for the job applied for. 'Resume' is also known as "curriculum vitae" or "bio-data". When you apply for a position in a business organization or a government office or anywhere else you are supposed to send all the relevant information about you – information including your academic record, personal achievements to justify your suitability for the post.

## IMPORTANCE

The writing of a good resume is very important. It is the first but very important step towards placement. It is the basis for shortlisting candidates for a written examination or an interview. A "resume" supplies a lot of information about a candidate's educational background, work experience calibre, communication skills; even his/her character to some extent and his/her habits. It helps your prospective employer to judge your potential. Of course a resume will not get you a job but you may be shortlisted for interview on the basis of it. So, due care must be given to the preparation of a "resume".

## ESSENCE OF A GOOD "RESUME"

(1) A good resume must have clarity of expression. The information contained in the "resume" should be organized logically and it should be complete. The "resume" must supply complete information about the candidate. It should contain only the relevant information.

Candidates should not mix styles or fonts in the "resume"

## WHAT CARE SHOULD BE TAKEN IN WRITING A RESUME?

(1) Candidates writing their "resume" should make sure that the information contained in the resume is truthful and based on facts and not on guesses or conjectures.
(2) The resume should be got neatly typed on paper of good quality.
(3) The resume should be free from any kind of mistakes of grammar or spelling. Remember, your resume is like your ambassador who represents you in your absence.

## WHAT SHOULD A "RESUME" CONTAIN?

A resume should contain the following information:

**Personal details:** It should mention your name, father's name, his profession, mother's name, her profession, your date of birth, age at present, present address, permanent address.

**Academic record:** It should give complete information about the examinations passed with percentage of marks/

grades, names of the universities/boards and years of passing. Academic record should be in reverse order.

**Schools/Institutions attended:** Resume should give a list of institutions attended by you.

**Details of extra-curricular activities:** An essential part of a resume is the enlistment of all extra-curricular activities in which the candidate participated during the course of studies. This information may include participation in seminars/workshops, debates, sports activities, organizational work, membership of N.C.C., N.S.S., etc.

**Hobbies/General interests, aptitudes:** The details about hobbies, general interests and aptitude should be mentioned in a resume.

**References:** Candidates are required to write the names, designations, addresses, telephone numbers and e-mail addresses of two prominent persons who can be referred to by the prospective employers for the verification of conduct and other details about the candidate.

**Profile:** Profile means a description of somebody that highlights his most important quality.

It may be written either at the beginning of the Resume or at its end.

## TYPES OF RESUME

There are three types of resume. They are:

(i) **Chronological, functional and hybrid.**
The choice of the resume depends on the specific job description.
**Chronological resume** is most suitable when you want to emphasize your excellence in academics and work experience. In the work experience category list your most recent experience describing your responsibilities and accomplishments.

(ii) The chronological type of resume is the most favoured type with the employers.

**Functional:** Functional type of resume is preferred by those applicants who are entering the job market or who want to redirect their career or who have little career related experience. The functional resume highlights the skills one brings to the job, especially his/her research and managerial experience which enables him/her to handle the position efficiently. In this type of resume the skill category gets the preference over work history and academic qualifications.

**Hybrid Resume:** Hybrid type of resume combines the best features of the chronological resume and functional resume. This type of resume is long and therefore it is not commonly used.

## SPECIMENS OF RESUME

### British Style

| | | |
|---|---|---|
| Name | : | Anil Sachdeva |
| Address | : | J-D 18 C Malvia Nagar, New Delhi |
| Telephone | : | (011)293596 |
| Mobile | : | 9312542787 |
| E-mail | : | as@stic.com |
| Nationality | : | Indian |
| Date of birth | : | 12 March 1989 |
| Profile | : | A well-trained highly educated young man with a creative and innovative mind. |
| Education | : | 2008-2012 Kota Technical University<br>B.Tech. in Computer Science Engineering (C.G.P. 9.5) |
| Languages known | : | English, Hindi and French |
| Extra-curricular activities | : | Participated in debates, seminars and organized activities/ cultural events. |
| Skills | : | Expert in preparing of design and DTP packages |
| Interests | : | Cricket, music and photography |

**REFERENCES**

1. Dr. C.B. Gupta,
   Head, Department of Computer Science,
   B.I.T.S., Pilani

2. Dr. O.P. Thakral,
   Dept. of Mathematics
   Thapar Institute of Engineering, Patiala

I enclose photocopies of my certificates.

**Signature**

---

**American Style**

R.C. RASTOGI
19 Panchsheel Marg,
New Delhi
e-mail rastogi@bits
telephone 011 (9341769)

**Objective:** To obtain a position as a Hindi-English translator with a firm in Gujarat, preferably in Ahmedabad

| | | |
|---|---|---|
| Date of Birth | : | 13 May, 1985 |
| Marital Status | : | Unmaried |
| Education | : | 2008-2010 P.G. Diploma in translation from Central Institute of English and Foreign Languages, Hyderabad<br>2006-2008 Master of Arts in English Literature from University of Rajasthan, Jaipur |
| Experience | : | 2010-Present Junior Translation Officer, Central Institute of Engineering Research, NOIDA (U.P.) |

| | | |
|---|---|---|
| | | 2008-2010 Junior translator, Bharat Heavy Electricals Ltd., Parliament Street, New Delhi. |
| Languages known | : | Fluent in English, French and Hindi |
| Personal interests | : | Reading literature and listening music |
| References | : | 1) Dr. V. Krishnamurthy,<br>Chairman,<br>Bharat Heavy Electricals Limited,<br>5 Parliament Street,<br>New Delhi - 210 015<br>2) Dr. P. Ramamurthy,<br>Director,<br>Central Institute of English and Foreign Languages,<br>Hyderabad- 397 015 |

*Specimen of resume for those persons who have excellent academic record, lot of research experience, a lot of published work and vast work experience seeking a position of challenges and great responsibility.*

---

## CURRICULUM VITAE

Dr. A. K. MALIK
Department of Mathematics
B. K. Birla Institute of Engineering &
Technology, Pilani (Rajasthan) 333031
**E-mail:** ajendermalik@gmail.com
**M. No:** 09887585785, 09784829785

### QUALIFICATIONS:

Ph.D. **Mathematics (Operations Research)**, from C.C.S. University, Meerut, (U.P.)

**Topic "Some optimum inventory policy for perishable items with two warehouses"**

M.Sc. **Mathematics** from G.K.V. Haridwar, (U.K.) in **Ist** division.

B.Sc. (**PCM**) from J.V. College Baraut, Baghpat (U.P.) in **Ist** division.

## WORK EXPERIENCE:

- Working as *Asst. Prof.* in the **Department of Mathematics, B. K. Birla Institute of Engineering & Technology, Pilani (Rajasthan)** since July 2, 2007.
- Worked as an *Academic Counseller* for **BCA** (Indira Gandhi National Open University) in **Birla Technical & Training Institute, Pilani (Rajasthan)** (IGNOU, SC/PSC - 23A0, PILANI) during the period Sep. 2010 to Dec. 2010.
- Worked as a *Lecturer* in the **Department of Mathematics, J. V. (P.G.) College, Baraut, Baghpat (U.P.)** from 26 Sep. 2005 to 28 Feb. 2007.

## RESEARCH AREA:

- Inventory Control Theory.
- Supply Chain Management.
- Soft Computing.
- Warehouses Management

## RESEARCH SUPERVISION:

- Guiding **two** students for their research work for the award of Ph.D. degrees.
- More than **20** students of B. Tech., P.G. and M.Phil. have completed their project work under me.

## COURSES TAUGHT:

- Calculus
- Engineering Mathematics-I,II,III,IV
- Discrete Mathematics Structure
- Real Analysis
- Linear Programming Problem
- Random Variable and Stochastic Process
- Computer oriented Numerical Methods
- Optimization Techniques

## PROFESSIONAL RECOGNITIONS:

- Reviewer of the journal "**Opsearch**".
- Editorial Board Member/Reviewer of the "**International Journal of Soft Computing and Engineering (IJSCE)**" ISSN: 2231-2307, Impact Factor (0.52).
- Editorial Board Member of the "**International Journal of Engineering and Advanced Technology (IJEAT)**" ISSN: 2249 - 8958, Impact Factor (0.24).
- Editorial Board Member of the "**International Journal of Recent Technology and Engineering (IJRTE)**" ISSN: 2277– 3878.
- Editorial Board Member of the "**International Journal of Physical Sciences**" ISSN: 0970-9150.
- Editorial Board Member of the "**International Journal of Mathematical Sciences**" ISSN: 0972-754X.
- Editorial Board Member of the "**American Journal of Mathematics and Sciences**" ISSN: 2230-8471.
- Editorial Board Member of the "**International Journal of Mathematical Sciences and Applications**" ISSN: 0976-3248.

- Member of international journal committee "**The Association for the Advancement in Combinatorial Sciences**".
- Editorial Board Member of the "**Bulletin of Society for Mathematical Services and Standards**" ISSN: 2277-8020.
- Worked as "**Organizing Secretary**" in a national seminar on "**Computational Mathematics & Operations Research**" during **28-29 November, 2009** in BK Birla Institute of Engineering & Technology, Pilani (Rajasthan).
- Life membership of journal of Rajasthan Ganita Parishad, "**Ganita Sandesh**" Ajmer (Rajasthan).

## BOOKS PUBLISHED:

1. **Engineering Mathematics I-** (New Age International (P) Ltd., New Delhi, INDIA), **2008.**
2. **Engineering Mathematics - II (**New Age International (P) Ltd., New Delhi, INDIA), **2008.**
3. **Mathematics (EC & EE) – III (**New Age International (P) Ltd., New Delhi, INDIA), **2009.**
4. **Advanced Engineering Mathematics - (**New Age International (P) Ltd., New Delhi, INDIA), **2009.**
5. **Random Variable and Stochastic Process - (**Neelkanth Publisher Ltd., Jaipur, Rajasthan, INDIA), **2011.**
6. **Mathematics (CS & IT) – III** (Asian Books Private Limited, New Delhi, INDIA), **2011.**
7. **Topology** (I. K. International Publishing House Pvt. Ltd., New Delhi, INDIA), **2012.**
8. **Optimization Techniques** (I. K. International Publishing House Pvt. Ltd.**,** New Delhi, INDIA) **2012.**
9. **Complex Analysis** (I. K. International Publishing House Pvt. Ltd., New Delhi, INDIA) **Forthcoming.**

10. **Mathematics for Engineering-IIT/BITSAT/AIEEE** (New Age International (P) Ltd., New Delhi, INDIA), **Forthcoming.**
11. **Operations Research** (Oxford University Press, New Delhi, India) **Work in progress.**

## PAPERS PUBLISHED IN JOURNALS:

1. **A. K. Malik, Yahveer Singh and S. K. Gupta (2012).** A Fuzzy Based Inventory Model for Deteriorating Items, **International Journal of Soft Computing and Engineering,** Vol. 2, No. 2, 188-192.
2. **S. R. Singh, A. K. Malik and S. K. Gupta (2011).** Two Warehouses Inventory Model with Partial Backordering and Multi-Variate Demand under Inflation, **International Journal of Operations Research and Optimization**, Vol. 2, No. 2, 371-384.
3. **S. R. Singh, A. K. Malik and S. K. Gupta (2011).** Two Warehouses Inventory Model for Non-Instantaneous Deteriorating Items With Stock-Dependent Demand, **International Transactions in Applied Sciences**, Vol. 3, No. 4, 749-760.
4. **A. K. Malik, Sanjay Kumar (2011).** Two Warehouses Inventory Model with Multi-Variate Demand Replenishment Cycles and Inflation, **International Journal of Physical Sciences,** Vol. 23, No. 3, 847-854.
5. **A. K. Malik, Yahveer Singh (2011).** An Inventory Model for Deteriorating Items with Soft Computing Techniques and Variable Demand, **International Journal of Soft Computing and Engineering,** Vol. 1, No. 5, 317-321.
6. **S. R. Singh, A. K. Malik (2011).** An Inventory Model with Stock-Dependent Demand with Two Storages Capacity for Non-Instantaneous Deteriorating Items, **International Journal of Mathematical Sciences and Applications,** Vol. 1, No. 3, 1255-1259.

7. **A. K. Malik, Ashu Sharma (2011).** An Inventory Model for Deteriorating Items with Multi-Variate Demand and Partial Backlogging Under Inflation, **International Journal of Mathematical Sciences,** Vol. 10, No. 3-4, 319-325.

8. **A. K. Malik, Ashu Sharma (2011).** A Two Warehouses Inventory Model for Linear Deterioration with Exponentially Demand Rate, **International Journal of Physical Sciences,** Vol. 23, No. 2, 577-784.

9. **A. K. Malik, Yahveer Singh (2011).** An Inventory Model for Deterioration Items with Variable Demand and Partial Backlogging, **International Journal of Physical Sciences,** Vol. 23, No. 2, 563-568.

10. **S. R. Singh, A. K. Malik (2010).** Two Storage Capacity Inventory Model with Demand Dependent Production and Partial Backlogging, **International Journal of Physical Sciences,** Vol. 22, No. 3, 795-802.

11. **A. K. Malik, Amandeep Singh, Simran Jit and C. P. Garg (2010).** Supply Chain Management-An Overview, **International Journal of Logistics and Supply Chain Management,** Vol. 2, No. 2, 97-101.

12. **C. B. Gupta, A. K. Malik and S. R Singh (2010).**A Two Warehouse Inventory Model for Deteriorating Items with Demand Dependent Production, **Ganita Sandesh,** Vol. 24, No. 1, 55-62.

13. **S. R. Singh, A. K. Malik (2010).** Inventory System for Decaying Items with Variable Holding Cost and Two Shops, **International Journal of Mathematical Sciences,** Vol. 9, No. 3-4, 489-511.

14. **S. R. Singh, A. K. Malik (2010).** Optimal Ordering Policy with Linear Deterioration, Exponential Demand and Two Storage Capacity, **International Journal of Mathematical Sciences,** Vol. 9, No. 3-4, 513-528.

15. **A. K. Malik, S. R. Singh and C. B. Gupta (2009).** Two Warehouse Inventory Model with Exponential Demand and Time-Dependent Backlogging Rate for

Deteriorating Items, **Ganita Sandesh** Vol. 23, No. 2, 121-130.

16. **S. R. Singh, A. K. Malik (2009).** Two Warehouses Model with Inflation Induced Demand under the Credit Period, **International Journal of Applied Mathematical Analysis and Applications,** Vol. 4, No.1, 59-70.
17. **S. R. Singh, A. K. Malik, (2008).** Effect of Inflation on Two Warehouse Production Inventory Systems with Exponential Demand and Variable Deterioration, **International Journal of Mathematics and Applications**, Vol. 2, No. 1-2, 141-149.
18. **A. K. Malik, S. R. Singh and C. B. Gupta (2008).** An Inventory Model for Deteriorating Items under FIFO Dispatching Policy with Two Warehouse and Time Dependent Demand, **Ganita Sandesh** Vol. 22, No. 1, 47-62.

## PAPERS PRESENTED IN SEMINARS/ CONFERENCES/SYMPOSIA:

1. **Two Warehouses Inventory Model for Non-Instantaneous Deteriorating Items with Stock-Dependent Demand** in **"CONIAPS XII"**12th Conference of the International Academy of Physical Sciences on **"Emerging Interfaces of Physical Sciences"**, December 22-24, 2010 organized by University of Rajasthan, Jaipur, India.
2. **An Inventory Model for Deteriorating Items with Two Warehouses and Demand Dependent Production** in 12th Conference of the International Academy of Physical Sciences on **"Emerging Interfaces of Physical Sciences"** December 22-24, 2010 organized by University of Rajasthan, Jaipur, India.
3. **Effect of Partial Backlogging with Exponential Demand and Demand Dependent Production on**

**Two Storage Capacity** in 80th Annual Session and National Symposium on "**Climate Change - Research, Awareness and Capacity Building**" December 2-4, 2010 organized by Jaipur National University, Jaipur (Rajasthan).

4. **Deterministic Inventory Model for Deteriorating Items with Seasonal Pattern Demand Rate and Shortages** in a national conference on **Recent Trends in the Advancement of Astronomy and Applied Mathematics** organized by Department of Mathematics SGRR (PG) College, Dehradun during 14 to15$^{th}$ November, 2009.
5. **An Inventory Model with Two Warehouses and Inflation Induced Demand under the Credit Period** in a U.G.C. sponsored national seminar on **Social Development under the Aegis of Operations Research** organized by Department of Mathematics Manohar Memorial Post Graduate College, Fatehabad (Haryana) on March 21-22$^{th}$, 2009.
6. **A Two-Warehouse Inventory Model for Decaying Items with Inflation and Partial Backordering** in 19$^{th}$ Annual Conference of Rajasthan Ganita Parishad & A symposium on **Numerical Techniques & Their Applications in Mathematics** organized by Department of Mathematics Jaipur Engineering College, Jaipur (Rajasthan) during January 18-19$^{th}$, 2008.
7. **A Two-Warehouse EOQ Model with Quadratic Demand Rate Without Shortage and Bulk Release Rule** in a national seminar organized by Department of Mathematics D.N. College, Meerut (U.P.) during 6$^{th}$ November, 2006.

## SEMINARS/CONFERENCES/WORKSHOPS ATTENTED:

1. An international workshop on **"Model Driven Engineering"** organized by ACM - BK Birla Institute of Engineering & Technology, Pilani (Rajasthan) during 27-30 March, 2012.
2. National conference on **"Modelling, Computational Fluid Dynamic & Operations Research"** organized by Department of Mathematics, Birla Institute of Technology & Science, Pilani (Rajasthan) during 4-5 February, 2012.
3. National workshop on **"National Workshop on Inventory Modelling"** organized by Center for Mathematical Sciences, Banasthali University, Banasthali sponsored by Department of Science and Technology, Govt. of India from 4-7 March, 2011 under the auspices of CMS.
4. **"3rd National Seminar on Recent Trends in Advancement of Mathematical and Physical Sciences"** organized by Department of Mathematics D.N. College, Meerut (U.P.) during 5-6 February, 2011.
5. National Conference on **"Emerging Dimension of Mathematical Sciences"** organized by Institute of Engineering & Technology, Alwar & Alwar Institute of Engineering & Technology, Alwer (Rajasthan) during 1-2 May 2010.
6. National Conference on **"Mathematical Modelling and Simulations"** held at Department of Mathematics, Guru Jambheshwar University of Science & Technology, Hisar (Haryana) during 20-21 March 2010.
7. National Workshop on **"Mathematical Modelling"** organized by Center for Mathematical Sciences, Banasthali University, Banasthali sponsored by Department of Science and Technology, Govt. of India from 15-16 December, 2009, under the auspices of Indian Mathematical Year, 2009.

## REFERENCES:

1. Dr. S. R. Singh
   Associate Professor
   D. N. (P.G.) College Meerut (U.P.)
   Mob. No. 9897682738
   Email: shivrajpundir@gmail.com

2. Dr. S. R. Yadav
   Retd. Professor
   Birla Institute of Technology & Science, Pilani
   Mob. No. 9413935833
   Email: sry1940@gmail.com

3. Dr. C. K. Jaggi
   Associate Professor
   Department of Operations Research
   Delhi University, Delhi
   Mob. No. 9891919399
   Email: ckjaggi@yahoo.com

## PERSONAL PROFILE:

| | | |
|---|---|---|
| **Father's Name** | : | Shri Virender Singh |
| **Date of Birth** | : | 01$^{th}$ February 1983 |
| **Sex** | : | Male |
| **Nationality** | : | Indian |
| **Languages known** | : | English & Hindi |
| **Marital Status** | : | Married |
| **Hobbies** | : | Playing Cricket, Listening Music. |

## DECLARATION:

I hereby declare that the information furnished above is true to the best of my knowledge.

**PLACE:** Pilani (Rajasthan) **(AJENDER KUMAR MALIK)**
2 May, 2012

## FORWARDING LETTER

A resume is accompanied with a forwarding letter. A forwarding letter should not include the information which is provided in the resume. It must refer to the source of information for the availability of the position and the applicant's interest for the job.

### TYPES OF COVERING LETTERS

#### Solicited Application Letter

A solicited application (covering letter) is written in response to an advertised post where the employer invites applications for a particular post mentioning the qualification and experience required for it.

#### Unsolicited Application Letter

This kind of letter is sent where the organization has not advertised the post.

#### Specimen of a Covering Letter (solicited)

The Director,
B.I.T.S.
Pilani
Sir,

With reference to your advertisement in the Hindustan Times of 23 March, 2012, I wish to be considered for a faculty position in the Department of Computer Science.

I am enclosing my resume for favour of your kind perusal and favourable consideration.

In case you need any further information, kindly let me know and I shall be glad to supply you the same.

Yours faithfully,

Signature
(R.C. Chaudhary)
15 D Ramesh Nagar, Jaipur

2 May, 2012
Encl: "Resume"

### Covering letter (unsolicited)

The Director,
B.E.T.
Pilani
Sir,
I have come to know through a friend of mine, who is working in one of your esteemed institutions, that you require some teachers in Mathematics for one of your schools. I am interested in this job and would feel grateful if given a chance to appear for a personal interview. I am enclosing a copy of my resume for your kind perusal.

Yours faithfully,

Dipika Nirmal
Ward No. 12
Near Hanuman Temple Pilani

2 May, 2012
Encl: "Resume"

### Some Useful Openers

1. I wish to apply for the post of a Lecturer in response to your advertisement in the Times of India of 16 March, 2012.
2. I have come to know from Dr. Rakesh Chaudhary, one of your faculty, that there are some posts of Lecturers lying vacant under your kind control.
3. Your advertisement in the Indian Express of 26$^{th}$ April has interested me as I have an aptitude for the kind of work involved in the job.

### Some Useful Closing Lines for Covering Letters

1. I would feel most thankful if I am given an opportunity of a personal interview.
2. I am looking forward to an opportunity of attending a personal interview.
3. With the kind of qualifications and experience I have got I think I can make the best use of my talent by working in an organization like yours.

# 15

# Business Letter Writing: Sales, Credit, Enquiry, Order, Claim, Complaint, Job Applications

## LEARNING OBJECTIVES

- To know the importance of letter writing for business organizations.
- To learn the principles of letter writing and to know about the various types of letters.
- How to write letters of credit, letters requesting credit, granting credit or refusing credit.

## IMPORTANCE OF LETTER WRITING

Letters are the oldest and most important means of communication. Inventions in the fields of science and technology have provided many other useful means of communication. Today we have phones, internet, fax, etc., which are the fastest means of communication at our disposal. In spite of these great inventions the importance of letter writing has not waned. Rather its importance has increased because of globalization, vast industrial growth, and expansion of business activities and advent of multinationals. Today we cannot conceive of any business activity without letter writing and organizations are giving more and more importance to the art of letter writing. Letters build the reputation of companies and ensure smooth and friendly relations between people.

A letter is a conversation through writing. Letters are used to communicate where either the electronic devices for communication are not available or they are too costly or the communication requires the confirmation of its receipt. Letters are the most important means of communication where it is necessary to keep records of communication.

Written communication has some advantages over verbal communication.

1. Communication through letters is precise and accurate because the writer of the letter has enough time to think, plan and revise the contents of his message.
2. Letters have the records of the dispatch and often acknowledgements are sought as confirmation of the receipt of the communication.
3. Copies of letters are kept as record of the communication which is not the case with verbal communication.

## TYPES OF LETTERS

We can divide the letters into two broad categories, i.e., personal letters and official letters.

**Personal letters** are written to friends, relatives and acquaintances. They have something personal to convey on a variety of subjects, like giving information, invitations, congratulations, expression of grief, etc. They convey feelings and emotions also. They are informal in nature and there is scope for the expression of emotions. Language of such letters is often colloquial and conversational.

**Business letters** deal with business affairs. They are concise and to the point. There is hardly any scope for the expression of feelings and emotions. The language is also formal.

Correspondence through letters is crucial for the successful functioning of an organization. Therefore organizations follow the following principles of letter writing.

## PRINCIPLES OF GOOD LETTER WRITING

1) **Courtesy/politeness:** Courtesy is the most important virtue of letter writing. Well written letters build the reputation of a company. It makes dealings smooth and helps to win friends. If a letter lacks courtesy we may lose both friends and business. Politeness costs nothing but it pays rich dividends. Sometimes we may receive a rude letter. To send a rude reply to a rude letter is not a good principle. If we send a polite reply to such a letter our correspondent may send us a polite letter. This is how companies build their goodwill by being very courteous in their correspondence. It is impossible to provoke good managers to be impolite.

### Some positive hints for a good start:

A good start is very important. You may start your letter with any of the following phrases to tide over a difficult situation:

(i) Indeed it is very nice of you to give your prompt attention to our communication.
(ii) We appreciate your kind consideration of our request.
(iii) Many thanks for your letter of 28 October, 2011.
(iv) We are glad to inform you that we have dispatched the garments you ordered vide your letter of .....
(v) Many thanks for your kind acceptance of our invitation/request.....

There are some phrases which irritate the reader. The following phrases should be avoided:

(i) We must remind you
(ii) We insist upon your making the payment in time
(iii) You are wrong in suggesting
(iv) Your complaint is absurd
(v) We cannot accede to your request
(vi) We are sorry to refuse ....

## Avoid the crowd approach/Avoid the passive voice

How you approach a person is very important. If you approach him as a friend you use the 'You approach'. If you approach him as a stranger or an unknown person, you apply the 'crowd approach'. Just study the following two sentences and judge yourself which one is friendly:

(i) This book will help **the readers** in understanding the day-to-day problems of life.

(ii) This book will help **you** in understanding the day-to-day problems of life.

The first sentence is addressed to some unknown person as if he is a stranger.

This is 'crowd approach'.

The second sentence is addressed to a person as if you know him intimately. It is a "you approach". Such an approach establishes good personal relationship.

2) **Avoid verbosity:** Verbosity means using more words than are necessary. Sometimes we use more words than necessary to make an impression or to please the addressee. This is a great defect in communication.

3) **Clichés, worn-out phrases should be avoided:** Some examples of verbosity are given below.

| VERBOSE | DIRECT AND CONCISE |
|---|---|
| As early as possible | Soon |
| At your earliest convenience | As early as you can |
| Beg to state | State |
| In early course | Soon |
| In the event of | If |
| Attached herewith | Attached |
| In compliance with your request | As requested |
| I would like to state | I state |

4) **Participle endings:** Participle endings as listed below hardly convey any meaning. They should be avoided.

(i) Assuring you of our best services at all times,

(ii) Looking forward to your favourable consideration of our request,

(iii) Hoping to hear from you soon,

**Clarity and precision:** Clarity and precision are the most important virtues of good writing. The communication must be accurate, precise and direct so that the reader gets the exact message without any kind of confusion or misunderstanding.

## STRUCTURE OF A GOOD BUSINESS LETTER

The following elements constitute the structure of a business letter.

(i) Heading/the name of the business organization and its address (it is printed on the letter pad.)

(ii) Date

(iii) Reference

(iv) Address of the firm to which the letter is sent

(v) Attention line (It gives the name/designation of the person whose attention is solicited

(vi) Subject

(vii) Body (contents of the letter)

(viii) Complimentary close

(ix) Signature

(x) Identification

**The above mentioned information is explained below.**

***Heading***

M/S Jai Prakash Nath & Sons,
Publishers and Booksellers,
Telephone No 23579
Lisari Gate,
Meerut

**Date:** 31 October, 2011

**Reference**: Your letter No. Ch/b/2931

### *Inside Address*

M/s Surjit Singh & Sons,
Booksellers,
Nai Sarak,
Delhi,

**Attention : Purchase Officer** - Mr. Khanna R.K.

Salutation:

Dear Sri Ram Kumar (formal)

My dear Ramesh (less formal)

**Subject:** Payment of our Bill No. 103 of 19 September for **the supply** of **books**

**Body:** Contents of the letters

### Complimentary Close

Complimentary close should be according to the salutation

| Salutation | Complimentary close |
|---|---|
| Dear Sir, | Yours faithfully, |
| Dear Sirs, | Yours truly, |
| My dear Singh, | Yours sincerely, |
| Dear Rakesh, | Yours sincerely, |
| Dear Member, | Yours sincerely, |
| Dear Reader, | Yours sincerely, |

Signature ( )

Mohan Lal,
Managing Director,
SLS

### Identification

Initials of the typist who typed the letter.

**Enclosures** A copy of the bill

**Difference between the British style of letter writing and the American style of letter writing:**

Major differences are:-

In the British style of letter writing the entries like complimentary close are on the right side of the paper. In case of American style of writing these entries are on the left hand side of the paper. In the American style of writing there is no indentation. In the British style indentation is used i.e., there is space before the para.

**Important subjects on which Business Houses exchange correspondence:**

(i) Sales
(ii) Credit
(iii) Enquiry
(iv) Order
(v) Claim
(vi) Complaint

## LETTERS OF SALE

How do business houses boost their sales? They do so through mass media advertisements. They use this media for promoting the items of mass consumption like bicycles, creams, tooth pastes etc. They also use personal contacts. This method of personal contacts has limitations because only a selected number of prospective buyers can be approached and it is very expensive. Most of the companies prefer contacts through correspondence. Through correspondence business houses can reach a large number of people and the cost is relatively low. Through these means they achieve a greater degree of success.

**How to make a sales letter interesting and effective?**

The introductory paragraph of a sales letter is very important. A good introductory paragraph can arrest the attention of the reader and he may feel tempted to read the whole letter. You can make your sales letter interesting by following some simple rules of writing good letters such as:

**(1) Making a striking statement like:**

(i) Do you want to feel young in old age?

(ii) Do graying hair frighten you?

(iii) Everyone wants to enjoy a sound sleep, you also do.

(iv) Everybody wants to look beautiful. You can do so at no great cost.

**(2) Emphasizing a significant fact:**

(i) Our ayurvedic medicine can keep away old age for a long time.

(ii) Our new shave lotion can give you a bright fresh face.

**(3) Telling a story, or an anecdote:**

Miss Mary was a very intelligent girl but was very shy. She suffered a lot from inferiority complex. She joined our professional courses. Where is she now? She is the Marketing Manager of a renowned company.

**(4) Special offers**

To attract customers the letter may also make special offers. It may also focus on the main selling point. The company may also offer discounts, guarantees, free trial offers and samples. All these temptations are offered through correspondence.

## SPECIMENS OF SALES LETTERS

### A sales letter for the promotion of an ayurvedic medicine

**Ayurvedic Medicine Limited**

NEW DELHI.

December 2, 2011.

Dear customer,

Do you want to look young in old age? Do wrinkles frighten you? Is graying a nightmare for you?

Now you needn't have any such fears. Our pharmaceutical company, after a long research, has discovered the secret of longevity hidden in the herbs of the Himalayas. They slow down the process of growing old and keep you fit and young. They have no side effects.

You can have these Live Young tablets from the chemists in your city or order them direct from us through correspondence or by dialing 93456.

Yours faithfully,

Marketing Manager

### Letter for promotion of the sale of mattresses

**Rakesh Household Goods Limited.**

Paharganj,
New Delhi.

2 October, 2012.

Dear customer,

Who does not want to enjoy a sound sleep after a day's hard work? Everyone does and so do you.

Our company has discovered a unique way to make nights pleasant through sound sleep. The mattresses manufactured by our company are soft and very comfortable. They are available in every town at affordable prices. Just give a ring at 93469 or write to us at the following address. You can avail the advantage of 10 per cent discount if you order the mattresses his by 30th December, 2012.

Hope you will take benefit of this unique offer.

Yours faithfully,

Manager

## CREDIT LETTERS

In business correspondence credit means an arrangement that you make with a business firm to pay later for something you buy today. Business houses offer goods on credit asking the customers to "buy now and pay later" to boost the sale of their goods. Buying and selling on credit has become the way of life for the wholesalers, retailers and consumers. This facility helps every one.

Selling on credit can be hazardous if sufficient care is not taken to find out the paying capacity of the buyers, their reputation, character and reliability.

There are three kinds of credit letters. They are:

(i) Letters seeking the facility of credit, i.e., buying things on credit,

(ii) Letters accepting the request for credit.

(iii) Letters rejecting the request for credit.

### Contents of the letter of credit

A letter requesting credit facility should have:

(i) Introduction of the firm seeking credit

(ii) The source of information about the company from which credit facility is sought

(iii) The placing of the order

(iv) Credit references.

### Contents of the letter of acceptance

(i) It should straightaway inform about the grant of credit facility

(ii) Satisfaction about the references

(iii) Terms and conditions of the credit facility, i.e., the maximum limit of the credit and the time limit within which the payment is to be made.

### Letters of rejection

(i) Thanks for showing interest in the goods

(ii) Regret for not accepting the request for credit facility.

(iii) Suggestions for buying on cash payment.
(iv) Assurance of credit facility in future

### Letter for the grant of credit facility for the purchase of books

**Sardar Kartar Singh & Sons**
Nai Sarak,
Delhi.
12 March, 2011

Messrs Jai Prakash Nath & Co.,
Subash Bazar,
Meerut City.
Subject : Order for supply of books on technical subjects.

Dear Sirs,
Ours is an old and well established firm dealing in purchase and sale of books on technical subjects. Messrs Punjab Book House, who are your old customers in Delhi, have informed us about your publications. They have also informed us that you provide credit facility giving a period of thirty days for payment after the supply of books.

We shall feel thankful if you kindly send us the following books on 30 days credit. We would also like to have similar credit facility for our future purchases. We promise to make payment of the bills within the stipulated period of 30 days,

1) Engineering Mathematics — Dr. A. K. Mallik, 30 copies
2) Inventory Control — Dr. A. K. Mallik, 50 copies
3) Mechanics — Dr. A. K. Mallik, 30 copies

I am giving the details of references who may be approached by you to vouch for our credibility.

Should you need my further information, we shall be glad to supply the same.

**REFERENCES**

1. Punjab Book House,
   Nai sarak, Delhi.
2. State Bank of India,
   Chandni Chowk, Delhi.

Yours faithfully

S Kartar Singh,
Proprictor

**Letter accepting the request for credit facility**

**M/S Jai Prakash Nath and Sons**

Subash Bazar,
Meerut City.

20 March, 2011

Sardar Kartar Singh & Sons,
Nai Sarak,
Delhi.
Subject: Supply of books on credit.

Dear Sirs,
We thank you for your letter of 12 March for supply of books on credit. We are glad to provide you credit facility for all purchases to be made by you.

We are satisfied with the references provided by you. We have already dispatched the books ordered by you and we hope you will receive them soon. We are enclosing the bill for the supply of books and we hope to receive the payment within the stipulated period of 30 days.

We assure you of our best services at all times,

Yours faithfully,
Manager

Encl.: Bill

### Letter rejecting the request for credit facility

**Unique Enterprises**
Kashmiri Gate,
Delhi.

12 May, 2012

Messrs Rajbir & Co.,
Bus Stop,
Pilani

Subject: Supply of leather goods on credit.

Dear Sirs,

We thank you very much for your letter of 3 May, 2012 showing your interest in the purchase of our leather goods. However, we regret to say that at present we are not in a position to supply you goods on credit.

We have fixed some limit for the grant of credit facility and we have already reached that limit. We shall be very glad to provide you this facility in the near future when it becomes feasible for us to do so.

We shall appreciate very much if in the meantime you make your purchases on cash terms and give us a chance to serve your interests.

Yours faithfully,

For **UNIQUE ENTERPRISES**

### Letters of Enquiry

Some letters are written to seek information, advice, direction etc. While writing such letters one should be careful not to ask for information which can be gathered from libraries or other sources. A letter of enquiry should be a brief one.

There are two kinds of enquiry letters. Solicited letters are written in response to some advertisements or notices where you want some further information.

Unsolicited enquiry letters are not in response to any advertisement.

Suppose you read a report in some magazine or you come to know of some product from your own sources and you want to know more about the product you write a letter. This kind of letter is an unsolicited kind of enquiry letter.

**Solicited enquiry letter**

March 2, 2012

**Messrs Thomson and Sons**
Mall Road,
Calcutta

Subject : Black Rose Herbal Cream

Dear Sirs,

We have been very much impressed by your advertisement in various newspapers of repute about the benefits of Black Rose Herbal Cream manufactured by your company. We would like to know further about this useful product especially its composition.

As the winter is approaching there will be great demand for creams.

We shall feel most grateful if you send us complete details about this product and also your trade terms.

Yours faithfully,

For Kapoor Novelty Store,
Jaipur.

### Unsolicited enquiry letter

**New Ways Leather House**
M.G. Road,
Bangalore.

2 March, 2011

**Messrs National Leather Products Limited,**
Cross Road,
Chennai.

**Sale of Leather Products**

Dear Sirs,

We have learnt from a business house of repute that your firm is actively engaged in the manufacture of leather goods like shoes, handbags, gloves etc. We are interested in the purchase of leather goods since we own a shop selling leather goods in Bangalore.

There is a great demand for leather goods from the student fraternity. It is a well known fact that Bangalore is one of the biggest educational centres in India and student community has craze for beautiful and fascinating products.

We shall feel most grateful if you kindly send us details of all the leather products manufactured by your company along with your trade terms.

We look forward to your prompt attention to our request,

Yours faithfully,

Proprietor

## Letters of Complaints and Claims

Business transactions take place between people. Often it is an act of buying and selling. Sometimes you are dissatisfied with the products or services supplied by the company. The goods supplied are not according to the sample. They do not meet with the specifications provided by you or the goods have been received in damaged condition. In such cases though you can make a complaint on phone, it is always better to write a complaint letter and if your company has suffered financial loss, you can ask for a claim.

Make sure that your letter of claim or complaint must be very polite. It is possible that the damage of goods or delay in delivery might have been caused unintentionally due to some common human error or to circumstances beyond human control.

There can be so many reasons for claims and complaints. Some of these are:

1) Goods supplied do not meet with the specifications supplied by you.
2) Goods have been damaged due to faulty packing.
3) Goods are not according to the samples provided by the company.
4) Goods have been received late.
5) Goods are of poor quality.
6) Error in billing

**Facts to be kept in mind while making complaints:**

1) A complaint should be written as soon as the mistake is detected.
2) The language of the letter of complaint must be very polite.
3) The complaint must be based on facts.
4) While writing a complaint all relevant information regarding consignment number, reference, the type of mistake, defect, shortage, delay, etc., must be given.

**Samples of a claim/complaint letter**

## Birla Public School

Pilani.

2 October, 2011.

**Messrs John & Sons**
Connaught Place,
New Delhi.

Subject : Supply of blankets

Dear Sirs,

Yesterday we received the consignment of blankets sent by you in response to our order of 23 August, 2011. On checking it we found that the consignment was short of ten blankets. We had ordered 200 blankets, while there were only 190 blankets in the consignment. Moreover, 40 blankets were found defective with faded colour. We are returning these forty blankets for replacement. Kindly send us 50 blankets of good quality soon.

As the winter season is approaching fast, we shall appreciate it very much if you give your prompt attention to our request and send us the blankets soon.

Yours faithfully,

For Principal

## Letter acknowledging the complaint letter

**Messrs John & Sons**
Connaught Place,
New Delhi.

12 November, 2011.

**The Principal**
B.P.S.
Pilani

Subject : Supply of blankets

Dear Sir,

We thank you for your kind letter of 2 October, 2011. We have received the 40 blankets sent by you.

We regret very much the discrepancy in the supply of blankets. We are sorry that some defective blankets were dispatched in the consignment. We are sending you a consignment of 50 blankets of good quality.

We are really sorry for the inconvenience caused to you. We have taken remedial steps in our Sales Department and in future you will never have any cause of complaint.

We assure you of our best services at all times.

Yours faithfully,

For John and Sons

Manager

## Claim Letter

**Navodaya Vidyalaya**
Jaipur.

2nd March, 2011.

**Messrs Cambridge School Products Ltd.,**
Karol Bagh,
New Delhi

Subject: Supply of School Bags.

Dear Sirs,

We had ordered 250 school bags for our students trusting the goodwill and reputation of your company. However, we find that the bags supplied by you do not match the samples supplied by you with your quotation.

Since the return of the bags and ordering of fresh supply of bags will take a lot of time and our new session has already started, we have decided to keep the bags. We, however, request you to accept our claim for suitable discount on the bags supplied.

We hope, keeping in mind the future business relationship, you will allow us a suitable rebate. We are returning your bill to enable you to make necessary corrections.

Yours faithfully,

Bursar,

For Navodaya Vidyalaya, Jaipur

### Letter accepting the claim

**Cambridge School Products**

Karol Bagh,
New Delhi.

10 March, 2011.

**The Bursar,**
Navodaya Vidyalaya
Jaipur

Subject : Supply of school bags

Dear Sir,

We are sorry to know that you are not satisfied with the quality of bags supplied by us. We had sent the bags of the best quality and we had taken special care with the dispatch of the consignment.

However, keeping in view our long-standing business relationship with you, we have accepted your claim and as a special case we are allowing you a ten per cent discount on this consignment.

We are sending you our fresh bill and we hope you will expedite its payment. We regret the inconvenience caused to you.

Yours faithfully,

Manager,

Cambridge School Products.

## Job Applications

When you apply for a job you offer your services to your prospective employer. Before you decide to apply you make sure that you fulfil all the qualifications and experience that your employer thinks are essential for the job. You also consider whether the compensation offered is according to your expectations. You also consider what other facilities like housing, transportation, etc., are being offered.

Once you make up your mind that the position meets with your expectations, you write your application giving complete details about your qualifications, experience, etc., in support of your candidature.

Nowadays applicants prefer to write their resume (also called curriculum vitae) and send it along with a covering letter.

Earlier, there used to be only one application letter containing all the information of the covering letter as well as resume.

There are two kinds of such application letters depending upon the source of information about the availability of the position. The source of information may be the advertisements inserted in the newspapers or it may be through a personal friend or acquaintance.

**The two types of job applications are given here:**

The Director,
Central Electronics Engineering Research Institute,
Chandigarh.

Application for the post of Scientist C

Sir,

In response to your advertisement appeared in the Hindustan Times of 5 November, 2012 inviting applications for the posts of Scientists in your esteemed institute, I wish to be considered for one of these positions.

I am giving below details of my educational qualifications, work experience, research experience and profile for favour of your kind consideration.

| | | |
|---|---|---|
| Name | : | Anurag Gupta |
| Father's name | : | Shri Shalesh Gupta |
| Father's occupation | : | Teaching -<br>Working as Professor in the Department of Computer Science, B.I.T.S., Pilani |
| Mother's name | : | Mrs. Shalini Gupta |
| Mother's occupation | : | Working as a teacher in Birla Balika Vidyapeeth, Pilani |
| Date of birth | : | 22 October, 1985 |
| Age at present | : | 27 years |
| Place of birth | : | Pilani |
| Present address | : | E202, Vidya Vihar, Pilani. |
| Permanent address | : | C-29, Vidyadhar Nagar, Jaipur |
| Nationality | : | Indian |
| Marital status | : | Unmarried |
| Examinations Passed | : | 2008-2010<br>M.Tech, Computer Science<br>BITS,Pilani C.G.P. 9.7<br>2004-2008 C.G.P. 9.6<br>B.Tech,. Computer Science<br>B.K.Birla Institute of Engineering Technology, Pilani |
| Special interests | : | (i) Listening music<br>(ii) Reading literature |

References : (i) Dr. Dalip Singh
Department of Computer
Science, B.I.T.S., Pilani
(ii) Dr. R. Solanki,
Dean,
B.K.B.I.E.T., Pilani

I am enclosing photostat copies of all my certificates and testimonials for reference.

If you need any further information, I shall be glad to supply the same on hearing from you.

Yours faithfully,

(Anurag Gupta)

Encls: Copies of testimonials

### Second Type of Application Letter

2 March, 2012.

The Director,
B.R.C.M. Engineering College,
Bahal (Haryana)

**Application for a faculty position**

Sir,

I have come to know from Dr. R.P. Gupta, a faculty member in your esteemed institution, that you are looking for suitable persons for faculty positions in the Department of Computer Science. I wish to be considered for one of these positions.

As regards my suitability for the post applied for, I wish to inform you I have obtained M.Sc. degree in first class from the University of Rajasthan, Jaipur as a regular student.

I got first position in my B.Sc. as a regular student of Maharaja College, Jaipur.

During my studies I took part in debates and seminars. I attended a number of workshops organized by the College/University.

I am a young man of 25 years of age with passion for teaching and research work. I belong to a respectable family and my parents are also teachers. My father is working as a senior faculty member in B.I.T.S., Pilani and my mother is working as a senior teacher in Birla Shishu Vihar, Pilani.

I shall feel most thankful if you kindly accord me the opportunity of a personal interview.

Yours faithfully,

(Ravi Choudhry)

E-202, Vidya Vihar

Pilani.
September 2, 2012.

# 16

# E-mail Messages

## LEARNING OBJECTIVES

- To know the importance of electronic mail as a means of communication and its advantages over written communication.
- To learn the technique of writing an e-mails.

Today there are so many means of communication but sending messages by e-mail has become the most popular method. E-mail is the abbreviated form of "electronic mail". It is a method of sending and receiving of messages over electronic communication system. It is an informal mode of communication. It has some distinctive advantages over written communication. These advantages can be briefly summarized as under:

(i) Sending e-mail messages is the cheapest mode of communication. If you send a written message you have to spend a lot of money in getting the message typed and getting it dispatched. In the case of e-mail messages all this effort and expenditure is saved.

(ii) It is the fastest mode of communication. Written messages take days in reaching their destinations. E-mail messages take no time as they are quick and convenient.

iii) Sending messages through e-mail saves a lot of paper work and stationery.

iv) In the case of e-mail messages one can get quick response.

v) E-mail messages can be sent to a large number of people at the same instant.

## REVOLUTION IN COMMUNICATION SYSTEM

Electronic mails were in use in the late twentieth century but their use was very limited. Since the last decade there has been a great increase in the use of e-mail as a mode of communication. Most of the business communication is being done through e-mails. Almost all kinds of information like policies, programmes, apologies, errors in billing, reminders, etc., are being transmitted through e-mails. Electronic media has brought a revolution in business communication and conventional methods of communication are slowly becoming defunct. Paperless offices have become the norm.

There has been a great increase in the use of e-mail communication during the present decade. It has become the most favoured mode of communication.

## DISADVANTAGES OF E-MAILS

The greatest problem is the great increase in the number of e-mails in an office and the voluminous nature of the messages. Officials find it difficult to handle such a large number of e-mails.

There is also some problem in comprehending the messages sent through e-mails. People know how to use computer, internet, etc., but they have difficulty in drafting the messages accurately. Often the messages are imprecise and the reader has to search for the main idea. Sometimes the language used in the e-mail is full of jargon and acronyms with which the reader is not familiar. E-mails are drafted casually and they are written in a language which is too informal. Language of e-mails is often full of mistakes of spellings and grammar and there are so many abbreviations.

E-mails lack confidentiality, so one should know when to send a message through e-mail and when to send it through letters. In spite of its inherent weaknesses e-mail communication is still very popular and cannot be done away with.

## WHEN IS WRITTEN COMMUNICATION PREFERRED?

When you are launching or promoting a new project or service do not do so on e-mail. Business houses write formal letters while introducing a new service or product. Sending an e-mail in such cases will not be regarded as a sign of good etiquette. Letters introducing new products are well-planned and carefully written. E-mail messages are used for day-to-day business communication and they do not receive the same kind of attention as the written communication.

## HOW TO WRITE E-MAILS?

We are living in an age dominated by e-commerce where communication skills contribute a lot to the success of a business organization. So the language on your website must be precise and self-explanatory so that the reader should know what he wants to know. People first check out the company's website before developing further contacts.

Normally, we use e-mails for providing information, requiring information or seeking clarifications. While writing an e-mail always take into consideration what information the recipient of the e-mail expects from you. Think well of the contents of the message and choose the language which is clear and precise so that there is no room for misunderstanding and doubt.

## IMPORTANCE OF THE SUBJECT LINE

We are living in an age where business executives receive a large number of e-mails in a day and often they do not have much time to read all the e-mails. To make sure that your e-mail receives proper and prompt attention make your subject line attention - compelling. Also see that there are no vague abbreviations. Use of unfamiliar acronyms and abbreviations poses problems to the reader. He may get irritated and lose interest in the communication. Only common acronyms and abbreviations should be used in e-mails.

Organising the contents of an e-mail is also very important. An e-mail must start with an introductory paragraph. The second paragraph should give the details of the contents. The concluding paragraph should state the action or follow-up required.

In some ways e-mail messages are like face-to-face conversations. They are informal in nature, so the language in an e-mail is colloquial and conversational.

## IMPORTANT RULES FOR WRITING GOOD E-MAIL MESSAGES

1. As far as possible use short and simple sentences. Avoid long and involved sentences to make the message easily readable.
2. A good e-mail should have only one subject. Use a separate e-mail for each subject.
3. Politeness should be the watchword for business communication. Though there have been rapid changes in the means of communication due to great strides in engineering technology, the rules of etiquette have not changed. E-mails should be written in a polite language.

Use of capital letters has its use in written communication but e-mail messages are written in small letters.

### Use of acronyms

Use of acronyms and abbreviations has become very common. But this must be made judiciously. Only those acronyms and abbreviations should be used with which the reader is expected to be familiar. Otherwise they will create confusion and cause irritation.

An acronym is a word formed from the first letters of the words that make up the name of something. For example UNO is an acronym for United Nations Organisation. An abbreviation is a short form of a word. For example "st" is the abbreviation of the word "saint".

### Some common acronyms

| | |
|---|---|
| ASAP | As soon as possible |
| FYI | For your information |
| IOW | In other words |
| NRN | No reply necessary |
| TIA | Thanks in advance |
| TYVM | Thank you very much |

### Common abbreviations

| | |
|---|---|
| U | you |
| dt | date |
| lt. | letter |
| Asst. | Assistant |
| C/o | Care of |
| w.e.f | with effect from |
| w/r | with reference to |

Never leave double spacing between words. However, proper spacing between paragraphs makes readability easy. You may indent the paragraphs to make them easily identifiable.

An e-mail should not cause any irritation to the reader. It will cause irritation if the text has mistakes of spellings and grammar. E-mails which have mistakes of grammar and spelling cause loss of reputation, good will and also loss of business.

To make the e-mail message easy to comprehend use simple and short sentences. Use concrete words. If you have to choose between a simple and difficult word, choose the simple one.

Sometimes you do not know whether the recipient of the e-mail is male or female. In such cases use gender neutral language.

E-mails, faxes and memos are similar in style. E-mails between friends and colleagues are formal. Business e-mails may be either semi-formal or formal depending on the relationship between the sender and the receiver and what the message contains.

Some basic rules for writing e-mails

(i) You must be consistent in style. Don't vary between formal and informal style.

(ii) Remember to use paragraphs.

(iii) Keep the message short and to the point.

(iv) Use the subject line to summarize the point of the message. It will make the reader clear about the content.

## SPECIMENS OF E-MAILS

**1.**

To Anil Mehta
From R. Saxena
Date 2 August, 2012

Subject : **Meeting tonight**

Hi Anil

Sorry to say I'll be a bit late for the meeting tonight. My son is suffering from fever and I have an appointment with the doctor.

I hope to make it by 8.00 p.m.

**2.**

To apg.bkit.com
From akm.bits.com
Subject : **Supply of garments**

The garments you ordered last month for your students are ready for deiwery. I am giving a list of garments with their colours and sizes currently in stock.

Rahul Saxena

## QUESTIONS FOR DISCUSSION

(1) What do you understand by an e-mail? What are its advantages over written messages?
(2) What are the general principles for writing e-mails?
(3) You are writing to a firm for the first time for the promotion of your new products. Which means of communication will you prefer, e-mail or written communication? Give reasons for your answer.
(4) Write common acronyms and abbreviations used in e-mails.

# 17

# Telephone Etiquettes

## LEARNING OBJECTIVES

- To understand the importance of telephone as a means of communication.
- To understand the difference between face-to-face and telephone conversation.
- To know the difference between telephone conversation and conference calls.
- To learn some commonly used words and phrases in telephone conversation.

## COMMUNICATION THROUGH TELEPHONE CALLS: ITS IMPORTANCE

The present age is the age of rapid communication. There are so many means of communication at our disposal. Written communication has been the traditional mode of communication for a long time and it has not lost its relevance even today nor is it likely to lose it in future.

The invention of telephone brought a revolution in communication techniques. It is a great boon which has made man's life easy and comfortable. No other means of communication can take the place of telephone conversation. It has certain undeniable advantages over the other means of communication. In many cases communication through letter writing is not practicable. If you want an appointment with a doctor you do not write him a letter and wait for his response. You simply pick up your phone, dial his number, and get the appointment fixed. If you want to make an enquiry from the railway department you do not go to the department. You simply ring them up. Most of the business activities take place with the help of telephone. If you want to know the cost of a brand calculator you simply phone the dealer and know whatever you want to know about it. In a nutshell it may be said that though telephone conversation has its limitations yet for certain uses it cannot be replaced by any other means of communication.

## FACE-TO-FACE CONVERSATION AND CONVERSATION ON PHONE

In many ways talking on telephone is similar to face-to-face conversation. But there are certain differences also. In face-to-face conversation you have the following advantages:

(i) You smile to welcome and befriend the person you are talking to.
(ii) You shake hands with him which shows your warm reception.
(iii) You can see the reaction of your counterpart and deal with him accordingly.
(iv) You can use your body language to explain your point of view more emphatically.
(v) You can make eye-contact with your counterpart.

## HOW TO OVERCOME THE DISADVANTAGES OF CONVERSATION ON PHONE?

The above-mentioned advantages of face-to-face conversation are not available to the person talking on the telephone. However, these disadvantages can be overcome by following certain principles while talking on the phone:

(i) Be very polite to make up for the absence of facial expressions.
(ii) Speak at a very low speed so that the person on the other side can understand you easily.
(iii) Plan your conversation very carefully.

(iv) Speak a bit loudly so that the person you are talking to may not have any difficulty in hearing you.

You can acquire perfection in the art of making conversation on phone. It requires some training and practice. To ensure the success of your conversation on phone plan your phone calls in advance. Prepare notes for the message to be conveyed. Master the technique of expression especially modulation of voice.

## LANGUAGE USED ON THE TELEPHONE

Language used on telephone is specialized. There are some common expressions which are used in various situations. These common expressions are:

(i) When you make a call you say:
**This is Anil speaking**

(ii) When you receive a call and the caller does not introduce himself you say:
**May I know who is speaking?**

(iii) When you dial a number and you do not find the man whom you want to talk to you say:
**Can I speak to Mr./Miss**

or

**I'd like to speak to Mr./Miss**

(iv) If there is an extension service and the person you want to talks is available on some extension you say:
**Please connect me to ........**

(v) If you receive a request on phone to connect him/her to somebody you say:
**Hold on a moment, please.**

(vi) Suppose you receive a call for somebody and he is not available you say:
**I'm sorry Mr. ____ is not available at the moment.**

(vii) The person you want to talk to is not available you may ask:
**"Could you tell me when he is likely to come?"**
You may get a reply:

**"Not until this evening"**
You can make a request like:

**Can you please ask him to give me a call ? My phone number is .........**
You may get the reply:

**I'll give him your message.**

or

You may say:
**"Can I leave a message for him?"**

## SPECIMENS OF TELEPHONE CALLS

### 1. Telephonic conversation with a nursing home

| | |
|---|---|
| Mohan | Hello, I am Mohan Kumar, Can I talk to Dr. Prashant Gupta? |
| Receptionist | I'm sorry Dr. Gupta is not available at the moment. I'm the receptionist. What can I do for you? |
| Mohan | My son is not feeling well. I want an appointment with him. |
| Receptionist | Well, he is likely to be available in the afternoon. |
| Mohan | Can you please get me an appointment with Dr. Gupta and give me a ring. |
| Receptionist | Certainly, Please give me your phone number. |
| Mohan | My phone No is 2420045. Thank you very much. |

### 2. Making an enquiry from the airport

| | |
|---|---|
| Rakesh | Good morning. Are you speaking from the airport enquiry? |
| Receptionist | Yes. I am from the airport enquiry. What can I do for you? |
| Rakesh | Can you tell me the status of flight number 205 from Dubai. Its scheduled time of arrival is 6.00 p.m. |
| Receptionist | Wait a minute, please. The flight from Dubai is fifteen minutes late. |
| Rakesh | I see, and what about the Indian Airlines flight to Mumbai. |
| Receptionist | It is scheduled to take off at 5 p.m. |
| Rakesh | Thank you. |

## IMPORTANCE OF COURTESY

Some people while interacting on phone use very polite and friendly expressions. In this way they make friends and achieve the desired results easily. Use of friendly expressions is very important and equally important is the tone of the voice. This also requires training and practice in voice modulation and companies while making appointments give due consideration to the ability of the applicants to use language effectively. To convey the same message you can choose different expressions – some very friendly and polite and some rough and unfriendly. Some specimens of these expressions are given below.

| Unfriendly and impolite | Friendly and polite |
|---|---|
| 1. Hold on. | Could you please hold on the line? |
| 2. Mr. Gray is not here at present. Call later. | Mr. Gray is not available at the moment. Could you please call a little later or leave a message. |

| | |
|---|---|
| 3. Put me through to the Principal. | Can I talk to the Principal, please. |
| 4. Tell Mr. Mohan that tomorrow's meeting is cancelled. | Could you please tell Mr. Mohan that tomorrow's meeting has been cancelled. |
| 5. Connect me to extension 549. | Could you please connect me to extension 549. |

## MAKING A CONFERENCE CALL

A conference call is like holding a meeting on telephone. Through a conference call a caller can speak to several people at the same time. These calls have become important at workplaces because a lot of work is conducted with organizations operating at long distances. The present age is the age of multinationals, globalization and outsourcing. Conference through conference calls saves time, money and exertions of travelling. Rules for the conventional meetings and conference calls are the same. The same rules of etiquette are followed both at the regular meetings and meetings through conference calls. But some technical aspects need to be taken care of for conference calls.

In today's world business houses have to keep in touch with far away locations. In such circumstances communication through telephone calls has assumed greater importance. Even more important are the inter-company conferences. They are taking the place of traditional conferences. Important decisions can be taken after consultations on phone and information can be transmitted quickly and cheaply.

Conferences through telephone calls can be made a smooth going affair by taking some precautions. During telephone conferences it should be made certain that there is no background noise and there are no interruptions. Breathing into the mouthpiece can be disruptive, so it must be avoided. Even taking notes via a computer keyboard may cause disruption.

If you want to make your telephone conference successful, do not use computer-based dial up system. Use the hand-held receiver for speaking. Avoid cell-phones and do not make a call from a moving vehicle.

Punctuality is very important for the success of a telephone conference. Call the given number at the exact time. Stick to the agenda of the conference and your conference call will be quite successful.

## QUESTIONS FOR DISCUSSION

1. Discuss the importance of communication through telephone for a business organization.
2. How is face-to-face conversation different from a telephone conversation?
3. How can a conversation on telephone be made as smooth and effective as the face-to-face conversation?
4. How can a conference call be made as smooth and effective as the traditional conference?

# PART II

## (Language Lab)

# 18

# Phonetic Symbols and Transcriptions

## Phonetic transcription

What is phonetic transcription?

Phonetic transcription means representation of English sounds through symbols.

### *Eaxmple*

Play plei

The word play has three sounds

(i) P (ii) l (iii) vowel ei

These three sound have been represented through symbols.

## Why learning of phonetic transcription is necessary?

(1) If we want to pronounce English words correctly we must have knowledge of phonetic symbols and practice in phonetic transcription.

(2) The spellings of English words are not based on sound. The sound of English words is not based on spellings. This is why learning of phonetic transcription is necessary for the correct pronunciation of English words.

## Consonant sounds

| Sound | Symbol | Examples |
|---|---|---|
| B | \| b \| | Bill, rob, bit |
| T | \| t \| | Tea, bit, rating |
| D | \| d \| | Day, red, madden |
| D | \| ∂ \| | This, bathe, with |
| Th | \| θ \| | Thick, earth, path |
| ch | \| tζ \| | Chain, church, reached |
| j/g | \| dz \| | Judge, jail, urge |
| sh | \| ʃ \| | Shoe, shilling, push |
| f | \| f \| | Fail, rough, refill |
| G | \| g \| | Go, gain, wig |
| H | \| h \| | Hat, hit, hoot |
| K | \| k \| | Kite, cool, king |
| l | \| l \| | Light, lay, lamp |
| M | \| m \| | Moon, room, roaming |
| N | \| n\| | Night, noon, mining |
| r | \| r \| | Rat, ring, rule |
| S | \| s \| | Say, kiss, miss |
| Z | \| z | Zoo, was, zen |
| V | \| v \| | Move, vest, love |
| W | \| w \| | Wet, water, woman |
| Y | \| j \| | Yes, yell, young |

## 12 vowel sounds

| | |
|---|---|
| I | Ill, is, nil, kill, mill |
| I: | Eat, ease, feel, meal, deal |
| U | Book, took, shook, nook |
| U: | Ooze, lose, loot, boot, move |
| ^ | Up, us, but, cut, rough |
| ∂ | Ago, again, afar, along |
| a: | Car, park, mar, ask, palm calm |
| e | Bet, met, set, red, fed, said |
| æ | Bat, mat, sat, fat, lad, mad |
| ⊃ | Pot, lot, go, rob, shot, shop |
| ⊃: | Law, saw, ball, call, walk |

| Two-vowel sounds (diphthongs) | |
|---|---|
| ei | Pay, may, aid |
| OU | Go, show, load, road, note, goat |
| ai | My, tie, sign, ice, eyes, mine, time |
| au | Out, mouth, loud, allowed |
| ⊃i | Boy, toy, coy |
| I∂ | Fear, dear, near, ear, mere |
| e∂ | There, mare, care |
| u∂ | Poor, tour, sure |

1. Phonetic transcription of words of one syllable

| | |
|---|---|
| It | it |
| Eat | i:t |
| Push | puʃ |
| Moot | mU:t |
| Bet | bet |
| Bait | beit |
| Pot | p⊃t |
| Law | ⊃: |
| Up | ^p |
| Car | ka: |
| Go | g∂u |
| May | mei |
| My | mai |
| Ear | i:∂ |
| Poor | pu∂ |
| Air | e∂ |
| Share | ʃe∂ |

## STRESS SYSTEM

### What is stress system?

English speech has rhythm. It has music. This rhythm is created by alternating stressed syllables and unstressed syllables. It means some syllables are stressed, i.e., spoken with greater breath force. Greater breath force is used for the production of stressed syllables. For example, the word 'receive' has two syllables 're' and 'ceive'. This alternating of stressed sounds and unstressed sounds gives rhythm to English speech. Words of one syllable spoken in isolation (not in speech) are not stressed.

**I. Mark the stress at the right place in the following words:**

1. Clever
2. Balloon
3. Admission
4. Collector
5. Already
6. Hospital
7. Exact
8. Random
9. Kingship
10. Nationality
11. Modern

## Solutions

1. 'Clever
2. Ba'lloon
3. Ad'mission
4. Co'llector
5. Al'ready
6. 'Hospital
7. Ex'act
8. 'Random
9. 'Kingship
10. Natio'nality
11. 'Modern

**II. Some examples of words with two syllables. Accent is on the first syllable.**

'Able
'After
'Agent
'Any
'Artist
'Holy
'Eager
'Butter
'Colour
'Body

## Accent on the second syllable

Words starting with weak prefixes are stressed on the second syllable.

A'bout
Ad'mit
A'go
Ap'point
Al'though
Be'gin
Be'lieve
De'fend
Po'ssess
Re'ceive

**III. Words of three syllables**

**a. Primary accent on the first syllable**

'Agency
'Article
'Bitterness
'Citizen
'Easily

b. **Primary accent on the second syllable**
A'greement
A'ppointment
A'ttention
Con'nection
Di'rector

**Primary accent on the second syllable**
After'noon
De'compose
Recom'mended
Seven'teen
Under'stand

# 19

# Word Formation

For the enrichment of your language you need to know words, i.e., you need to enrich your word power and to know how to use these words correctly in sentences. You also need to learn the formation of sentences, i.e., to learn the basic structures of sentences. The present chapter deals with the ways to enrich your word power, i.e., to develop your vocabulary.

There are two kinds of words. They are called 'root' words and 'derivatives'.

## ROOT WORD

A root word is the word that has the main meaning and other forms are based on it. It is a word that other words are formed from. For example "walk" is the root word of 'walking' "walked" "walks". A root word is also called a primary word or a base word. It cannot be divided.

### Derivatives

A derivative word is a word that has been developed from another word. For example the word "happiness" is the derivative of the word "happy". Derivatives are also called complex words.

### How to form derivatives?

We can form derivatives by:

(i) Using prefixes
(ii) Adding suffixes
(iii) Making compound words by joining two root words.

### Use of prefixes

Prefixes are added before the root words. For example, we add "en" before "able" to make it "enable".

Suffixes are added at the end of words. For example we add 'ful' after "faith" to make it "faithful". Compound words are made by joining two root words like 'foot-path'.

### Use of negative prefixes

We use the following negative prefixes to make antonyms.

#### *Use of prefix "de"*

| Root word | Derivative |
|---|---|
| Classify | declassify |
| Criminalize | de-criminalize |
| Stabilize | destabilize |
| Throne | dethrone |
| Centralize | decentralize |

#### *Use of prefix 'un'*

| | |
|---|---|
| Known | unknown |
| Acceptable | unacceptable |
| Accountable | unaccountable |
| Affected | unaffected |
| Happy | unhappy |
| Certainly | uncertainly |

#### *Prefix "dis"*

| | |
|---|---|
| Obey | disobey |
| Associate | disassociate |
| Honourable | dishonourable |
| Interested | disinterested |

| | |
|---|---|
| Loyal | disloyal |
| Order | disorder |
| Qualify | disqualify |
| Tasteful | distasteful |
| Unity | disunity |
| Engage | disengage |

***Use of prefix "in"***

| | |
|---|---|
| Ability | inability |
| Applicable | inapplicable |
| Capable | incapable |
| Appropriate | inappropriate |
| Articulate | inarticulate |
| Audible | inaudible |

***Use of prefix 'im'***

| | |
|---|---|
| Moderate | immoderate |
| Mortal | immortal |
| Possible | impossible |
| Probable | improbable |

***Use of prefix "in"***

| | |
|---|---|
| Ability | inability |
| Accurate | inaccurate |
| Active | inactive |
| Advisable | inadvisable |
| Appropriate | inappropriate |
| Attentive | inattentive |
| Audible | inaudible |
| Capable | incapable |
| Comparable | incomparable |
| Correct | incorrect |

### Use of prefix "ir"

| | |
|---|---|
| Relevant | irrelevant |
| Regular | irregular |
| Rational | irrational |
| Responsible | irresponsible |
| Respective | irrespective |
| Repressible | irrepressible |
| Resistible | irresistible |
| Resolute | irresolute |
| Reversible | irreversible |

### Prefix "il"

| | |
|---|---|
| Legal | illegal |
| Legitimate | illegitimate |
| Legible | illegible |
| Literate | illiterate |
| Liberal | illiberal |

### Use of prefix "non", "mis" and "mal"

| | |
|---|---|
| Cooperation | non-cooperation |
| Violence | non-violence |
| Trust | mistrust |
| Behave | misbehave |
| Conduct | misconduct |
| Miscible | immiscible |
| Treatment | maltreatment |
| Practice | malpractice |

### Formation of verbs from nouns/adjectives

We form verbs from nouns/adjectives by prefixing "en"

| | |
|---|---|
| Force | enforce |
| Able | enable |
| Circle | encircle |
| Courage | encourage |

| | |
|---|---|
| Joy | enjoy |
| Large | enlarge |
| Slave | enslave |

***By using the prefix "em"***

| | |
|---|---|
| Body | embody |
| Power | empower |

***By using the prefix "be"***

| | |
|---|---|
| Fool | befool |
| Friend | befriend |
| Guile | beguile |

**Use of suffixes for formation of new words**

Various suffixes are used for changing the part of speech of words.

**Formation of nouns from verbs by using the suffix "ment"**

| Verbs | Nouns |
|---|---|
| Achieve | achievement |
| Advertise | advertisement |
| Amuse | amusement |
| Announce | announcement |
| Establish | establishment |
| Govern | government |
| Improve | improvement |
| Judge | judgement |
| Appoint | appointment |
| Assign | assignment |
| Commence | commencement |
| Develop | development |
| Disappoint | disappointment |
| Enjoy | enjoyment |

### *Use of suffixes "ance", "ence"*

| | |
|---|---|
| Accept | acceptance |
| Allow | allowance |
| Appear | appearance |
| Assist | assistance |
| Attend | attendance |
| Maintain | maintenance |
| Depend | dependence |
| Excel | excellence |
| Endure | endurance |
| Guide | guidance |
| Rely | reliance |
| Repent | repentance |
| Resist | resistance |

### *Use of the suffix "al"*

| | |
|---|---|
| Arrive | arrival |
| Bury | burial |
| Deny | denial |
| Dismiss | dismissal |
| Dispose | disposal |
| Propose | proposal |
| Refuse | refusal |
| Remove | removal |
| Survive | survival |

### *Use of suffix "ion"*

| | |
|---|---|
| Accommodate | accommodation |
| Act | action |
| Agitate | agitation |
| Calculate | calculation |
| Collect | collection |
| Construct | construction |
| Create | creation |

| | |
|---|---|
| Discuss | discussion |
| Distribute | distribution |
| Exhibit | exhibition |
| Imagine | imagination |
| Inspect | inspection |
| Elect | election |
| Except | exception |
| Illustrate | illustration |
| Imagine | imagination |
| Invent | invention |
| Invite | invitation |
| Irrigate | irrigation |
| Perfect | perfection |
| Prevent | prevention |
| Predict | prediction |
| Protect | protection |
| Recollect | recollection |
| Revise | revision |
| React | reaction |
| Separate | separation |
| Vacate | vacation |

**Formation of nouns from verbs with the suffix "sion"**

| Verbs | Nouns |
|---|---|
| Compel | compulsion |
| Conclude | conclusion |
| Expel | expulsion |
| Extend | extension |
| Include | inclusion |
| Convert | conversion |
| Decide | decision |
| Revise | revision |
| Suspend | suspension |

**Formation of nouns from verbs with the suffix "ssion"**

| Verbs | Nouns |
|---|---|
| Admit | admission |
| Omit | omission |
| Proceed | procession |
| Remit | remission |
| Submit | submission |

**Formation of nouns from verbs with the suffix "ption"**

| Verbs | Nouns |
|---|---|
| Absorb | absorption |
| Assume | assumption |
| Consume | consumption |
| Deceive | deception |
| Resume | resumption |
| Describe | description |

**Formation of nouns from verbs with the suffix "ation"**

| Verbs | Nouns |
|---|---|
| Administer | administration |
| Admire | admiration |
| Alter | alteration |
| Consider | consideration |
| Converse | conversation |
| Declare | declaration |
| Examine | examination |
| Expect | expectation |
| Form | formation |
| Inspire | inspiration |
| Occupy | occupation |
| Register | registration |

| | |
|---|---|
| Restore | restoration |
| Starve | starvation |
| Tempt | temptation |
| Transport | transportation |

**Other suffixes for the formation of nouns from verbs are:**

| | | |
|---|---|---|
| (i) | ition - | addition from add |
| (ii) | cation- | justification from justify |
| (iii) | 'y' - | assembly from assemble |
| (iv) | 'ery'- | discovery from discover |
| (v) | 'ure'- | failure from fail |
| (vi) | 'age'- | carriage from carry |

**Some more examples of formation of nouns from verbs**

| Verbs | Nouns |
|---|---|
| Abolish | abolition |
| Advise | advice |
| Analyse | analysis |
| Behave | behaviour |
| Believe | belief |
| Certify | certificate |
| Compare | comparison |
| Criticize | criticism |
| Obey | obedience |
| Offend | offence |
| Err | error |
| Feed | food |
| Fly | flight |
| Grieve | grief |
| Hate | hatred |
| Introduce | introduction |
| Know | knowledge |
| Laugh | laughter |
| Serve | service |

| | |
|---|---|
| Sing | song |
| Slay | slaughter |
| Solve | solution |
| Prosper | prosperity |
| Prove | proof |
| Pursue | pursuit |
| Resolve | resolution |
| Respond | response |
| Satisfy | satisfaction |
| Succeed | success |
| Suspect | suspicion |
| Vary | variety |

**Formation of nouns from adjectives**

(i) With the suffix **"ness"**

| Adjectives | Nouns |
|---|---|
| Bitter | bitterness |
| Calm | calmness |
| Clever | cleverness |
| Empty | emptiness |
| Fond | fondness |
| Great | greatness |
| Keen | keenness |
| Kind | kindness |
| Mean | meanness |
| Nervous | nervousness |
| Ready | readiness |
| Happy | happiness |
| Weak | weakness |
| Rich | richness |
| Sad | sadness |
| Selfish | selfishness |
| Sweet | sweetness |
| Wicked | wickedness |

## Formation of nouns with the suffix "ity"

| Adjective | Nouns |
|---|---|
| Active | activity |
| Dense | density |
| Extreme | extremity |
| Generous | generosity |
| Hostile | hostility |
| Inferior | inferiority |
| Intense | intensity |
| Mental | mentality |
| Noble | nobility |
| Popular | popularity |
| Pure | purity |
| Scarce | scarcity |
| Superior | superiority |
| Uniform | uniformity |
| Vital | vitality |

## Formation of verbs from nouns with the suffix "ize", "ise"

| Nouns | Verbs |
|---|---|
| Apology | apologize |
| Critic | criticize |
| Economy | economize |
| Harmony | harmonize |
| Memory | memorize |
| Patron | patronize |
| Utility | utilize |
| Victim | victimize |

## Formation of verbs from nouns with the suffix "ate"

| Nouns | Verbs |
|---|---|
| Captive | captivate |
| Facility | facilitate |

| | |
|---|---|
| Motive | motivate |
| Origin | originate |
| Table | tabulate |

**With the suffix "fy"**

| Nouns | Verbs |
|---|---|
| Beauty | beautify |
| Class | classify |
| Pure | purify |
| Fort | fortify |
| Glory | glorify |
| Terror | terrify |

**Formation of verbs from adjectives**

***With the suffix "en"***

| Adjectives | Verbs |
|---|---|
| Black | blacken |
| Bright | brighten |
| Dark | darken |
| Hard | harden |
| Sharp | sharpen |
| Soft | soften |
| Sweet | sweeten |
| White | whiten |

***With the suffix "ize/ise"***

| Adjectives | Verbs |
|---|---|
| Civil | civilize |
| Fertile | fertilize |
| Special | specialize |
| Stable | stabilize |

**Formation of adjectives from nouns with the suffix "al"**

| Nouns | Adjectives |
|---|---|
| Agriculture | agricultural |
| Brute | brutal |
| Centre | central |
| Education | educational |
| Globe | global |
| Magic | magical |
| Instrument | instrumental |
| Music | musical |
| Nation | national |
| Occasion | occasional |
| Person | personal |
| Season | seasonal |
| Tradition | traditional |
| Universe | universal |
| Verb | verbal |

***With the suffix 'ial'***

| Nouns | Adjectives |
|---|---|
| Ceremony | ceremonial |
| Commerce | commercial |
| Essence | essential |
| Office | official |
| President | presidential |
| Province | provincial |
| Resident | residential |

***With the suffix "ar"***

| Nouns | Adjectives |
|---|---|
| Muscle | muscular |
| Spectacle | spectacular |
| Table | tabular |

***With the suffix 'ful' and 'less'***

| Nouns | Adjectives |
|---|---|
| Beauty | beautiful |
| Care | careful |
| Fancy | fanciful |
| Force | forceful |
| Harm | harmful |
| Cheer | cheerful |
| Delight | delightful |
| Pain | painful |
| Peace | peaceful |
| Resource | resourceful |
| Revenge | revengeful |
| Use | useful |
| Wonder | wonderful |
| Faith | faithful |
| Harm | harmless |
| Shame | shameless |
| Use | useless |

***With the prefix "ours"***

| Nouns | Adjectives |
|---|---|
| Adventure | adventurous |
| Courage | courageous |
| Contempt | contemptuous |
| Danger | dangerous |
| Marvel | marvellous |
| Nerve | nervous |
| Poison | poisonous |
| Fame | famous |
| Fury | furious |
| Glory | glorious |
| Prosperity | prosperous |
| Victory | victorious |
| Virtue | virtuous |

**Adjectives are also formed from nouns by using the following suffixs**

| Suffix | Nouns | Adjectives |
|---|---|---|
| 'ious' | Space | spacious |
| 'ic' | Hero | heroic |
| 'ish' | Boy | boyish |
| 'd/ed' | Wretch | wretched |
| 'ern' | West | western |
| 'en' | Wood | wooden |
| 'ing' | Charm | charming |
| 'ate' | Passion | passionate |
| 'like' | Child | childlike |
| 'worthy' | Praise | praiseworthy |

**Formation of adjectives from verbs by suffixing "able" to the verbs**

| Verbs | Adjectives |
|---|---|
| Cure | curable |
| Desire | desirable |
| Enjoy | enjoyable |
| Use | usable |
| Work | workable |

**Formation of adverbs from adjectives**

Normally adverbs are formed by suffixing **"ly" to the adjectives**

| Adjectives | Adverbs |
|---|---|
| Able | ably |
| Brief | briefly |
| Careful | carefully |
| Easy | easily |
| Frequent | frequently |
| Immense | immensely |

| | |
|---|---|
| Kind | kindly |
| Necessary | necessarily |
| Obedient | obediently |
| Possible | possibly |
| Proper | properly |
| Punctual | punctually |
| Real | really |
| Secret | secretly |
| Short | shortly |
| Special | specially |
| Urgent | urgently |

# 20

# Affixes

There are two kinds of words – root words and derivatives, i.e., words derived from root words with the help of affixes. A root word is also called "free morpheme" and "affix" is called "bound morpheme".

A morpheme is the minimal unit in the grammatical system of language. Consider the structure of the word "unhappy". This word can be divided into two constituents (i) "un" and "happy". Units "un" and "happy" cannot be further divided. We can say that the word 'unhappy' consists of two morphemes "un" and "happy". They are minimal units as they cannot be further divided.

### *Example*

The word "unfit" has two morphemes "un" and "fit".

### Free morphemes (root words)

Morphemes are of two types. They are called "free morphemes" and "bound morphemes". Morphemes like "happy" "regard" can stand on their own as independent words. They have their meanings. Such morphemes are called "free morphemes" or "root" words.

### *Examples*

The underlined morphemes in the following words are free morphemes or root words:

(i) mis fit
(ii) un popular

### Bound Morphemes (Affixes)

Morphemes like "un", "dis", "ed", "ly", etc. cannot stand on their own as independent units. Such morphemes are called "bound morphemes". In grammatical language they are called "affixes".

#### *Examples*

The underlined morphemes in the following words are called bound morphemes, i.e., affixes

dis honest
il legitimate
design ed

### Affixes, prefixes, suffixes and stems

A bound morpheme is attached to a free morpheme. This bound morpheme is called "affix". The free morpheme to which it is attached is called stem (the root word). In the word "unhappy" "un" is an affix and "happy" is the root word.

### Prefixes and suffixes

Affixes can come in the beginning of words and at the end of words.

#### *Examples*

**(i) "Unfair"** In the word "unfair" "un" is coming in the beginning of the word. In the case of faithful "affix" "ful" is coming at the end of the word.

Affixes which are attached at the beginning of stems (root words) are called prefixes. The affixes in the following words are examples of prefixes.

| Prefix | Root word | Word |
|---|---|---|
| Dis | lodge | dislodge |
| Dis | parity | disparity |
| Dis | engage | disengage |
| Dis | agree | disagree |
| Dis | comfort | discomfort |
| Im | proper | improper |
| Im | mortal | immortal |
| Im | mobile | immobile |
| Ir | regular | irregular |
| Ir | relevant | irrelevant |

## Suffixes

Affixes which are attached at the end of stems (root words) are called **"suffixes"**

***Examples***

| Root words | Suffixes | Derivatives |
|---|---|---|
| Pain | ful | painful |
| Faith | ful | faithful |
| Need | ful | needful |
| Man | hood | manhood |
| Talk | ing | talking |
| Wrong | ly | wrongly |
| Decease | ed | deceased |
| Wrong | ed | wronged |

Some words have both prefixes and suffixes

***Examples***

| Words | Prefix | Suffix |
|---|---|---|
| Unprotected | un | ed |
| Irrespectively | ir | ly |
| Unmoving | un | ing |

| | | | |
|---|---|---|---|
| Unfairly | un | | ly |
| Dislodged | dis | | ed |
| Unceremoniously | un | | ly |
| Illogical | il | | al |
| Unperturbed | un | | ed |

# 21

# Listening and Speaking Skills

## LISTENING

The process of oraly communication involves speaking and listening. The success of communication depends on the ability of the speaker to communicate effectively. It equally depends on the listener's ability to receive the message smoothly. The process of listening involves receiving the message, interpreting it and responding to it. The listening process is very important in the exchange of communication but its importance is not properly understood. Most of the people think that listening is a natural process. But it is a fact that most of the people are not good listeners which results in the failure of effective communication. Listening is a skill that needs to be developed through training and practice.

## HEARING AND LISTENING

Most people think that hearing and listening are the same. They make no distinction between hearing and listening. Hearing solely depends on ears. It is a physical act. Hearing involves just receiving sound signals. We hear whether we are interested in hearing or not. Hearing is a passive act. On the other hand listening is an active process. It is a mental process. Listening is concerned with making sense or meaning of what we hear. Listening involves receiving the message and interpreting it.

## THE LISTENING PROCESS

The complete process of listening involves: (i) receiving the message; (ii) interpreting it; (iii) storing the message in the brain; (iv) interpreting the message; and (v) responding to it.

## TYPES OF LISTENING

Listening is concerned not only with receiving the messages and interpreting them. It has some other important functions to perform. There are several kinds of listening.

1. **Appreciative Listening**

   Often we get a lot of pleasure from listening. We get a lot of pleasure from listening music or recitation of poetry or even dialogues in a play or in a movie. This kind of listening is called appreciative listening.

2. **Empathetic Listening**

   Man is a social animal. He shares his feelings of joy and sorrow with others to get relief. We often console a friend in grief by speaking kind, soothing, and sympathetic words. This listening gives him relief. This kind of listening is called empathetic listening.

3. **Comprehensive Listening**

   Comprehensive Listening means listening and comprehending, what is being spoken. This kind of listening is needed by the students in the classrooms and by officials in the meetings where one has to listen attentively, comprehend the messages and respond to them.

4. **Evaluative Listening**

   In this kind of listening the listener judges and evaluates what is being said and expresses his approval or disapproval of it. This is also called critical listening.

## TRAITS OF A GOOD LISTENER

### Body Language

The listener should listen actively and he should also show through body language that he is listening with interest. The listener must maintain eye contact with the speaker to show that he is listening actively. He should also give verbal signs like nodding the head occasionally, smiling or through other facial expressions.

### Avoid distractions

Distractions hamper the smooth process of listening. In the meetings most of the distractions are caused by the ringing of mobile phones. When one is attending important meetings one should switch off the mobile phone. Looking at your watch, shuffling papers or moving uneasily in the chair also cause distractions and displease the speaker.

### Ask questions

If you ask questions the speaker will feel that you are listening to him attentively.

### Empathise with the speaker

Empathy means showing consideration to the speaker's point of view and appreciating it. This attitude of the listener encourages the speaker to communicate openly, frankly and honestly.

### Listen with an open mind

Sometimes one may find that the communication is not interesting. One may disagree with the views expressed by the speaker. Even in such situations a good listener does not lose his patience or temper. To remain cheerful, positive, calm and unperturbed are the characteristics of a good listener.

### Paraphrasing

If the listener wants to clarify a point he should restate in his own words what the speaker has said. He may seek clarifications by politely asking the speaker in words like:

(i) So you mean to say –

(ii) I guess you want to say –

### What do good listeners do?

(i) Good listeners prepare themselves mentally to listen.

(ii) They evaluate the speech, not the speaker.

(iii) They keep away any prejudices against the speaker. They depersonalize their feelings.

(iv) They focus on the speaker in a generous way.

(v) They overcome barriers and disruptions.

(vi) They concentrate too hard on the content of the message.

(vii) Listeners should not pay too much attention to the clothing and appearance of the speaker.

(viii) Empathising with the speaker is also a good trait of listeners. They should be considerate to him and should not be very harsh in their judgments.

## SPEAKING SKILLS

In the present world characterized by speed, efficiency and competition speaking skills have acquired greater importance. Speaking is the most important component of oral communication. Oral communication involves two persons, i.e., the sender (speaker) and the receiver (listener). Success of communication depends on the ability of the speaker to speak well as well as the ability of the listener to listen well. There is no profession worth the name where speaking skills are not required. If you are in the teaching profession your success depends on your speaking skills. If you are in the marketing division of a firm you have to deal with customers and convince them about the quality of your products, hence, your speaking power comes into play. If you are holding a leading position in industry, government department or army you need your speaking skills to motivate the members of your team.

Communication is verbal and non-verbal. Verbal communication makes use of words and sounds. Non-verbal communication is made through signs, gestures, body language. Verbal communication involves written communication and oral communication, i.e., speaking.

Oral communication, i.e., speaking is very important. Without the ability to speak we are like deaf and dumb persons. Oral communication is primary. Written language is secondary. It came first in the life of man. It is spoken even by illiterate persons. For day-to-day routine matters we use oral communication, i.e., we speak.

Speech has some more advantages over written language. While speaking the speaker can make use of his body language, gestures, and facial expressions to make his communication more effective. He can charm his audience with a sweet smile. In face-to-face conversation he can shake hands to establish friendly relations. On a round of the factory a manager can enthuse his workers by tapping them on the shoulders.

## HOW TO ACQUIRE SPEAKING SKILLS?

Speech is a natural phenomenon. A child learns it naturally by imitating the sounds it hears. A child starts speaking after about a year of its birth. But the ability to speak well, to communicate effectively, to speak in public requires a lot of training and practice.

### How does a child learn to speak?

There are four steps to language learning. These are:

(i) Listening

(ii) Speaking

(iii) Reading

(iv) Writing

As soon as a baby is born it starts listening. It is taking the first step to language learning. It is trying to listen and trying to imitate the sounds it hears.

After about a year of listening it tries to speak by imitating the sounds it hears. This is the second step to language learning.

When the baby is three or four years old it is taught to read the alphabet and words. This is the child's third step to language learning. Later he is taught how to write.

## ESSENCE OF GOOD SPEAKING

(i) To be able to speak well you need to have knowledge of more and more words, their meanings and how to use them. Increase your vocabulary (word power) as much as possible.

(ii) You must have mastery over the articulation of English sounds. There is often the influence of the mother tongue. So the knowledge how to articulate English sounds is very important. Knowledge of phonetics and phonetic transcription is important.

(iii) English is a rhythm based language. This rhythm is created by following the patterns of word stress and sentence stress. You need to know and practise intonation in your speech.

(iv) In spoken language the speaker has the advantage of making use of body language, gestures, signs, to make his speech effective and entertaining.

## HOW TO IMPROVE YOUR SPEAKING POWER

The best way of acquiring proficiency in speaking is through speaking. As you cannot learn horse riding without sitting on the back of a horse, as you cannot learn swimming without jumping into water, so you cannot learn speaking without speaking. Here are some tips for you to master the art of speaking.

(i) Speaking is learnt through imitation. Listen as much well spoken English as possible. If you are a student listen to the lectures delivered by your teachers attentively. You can listen the English news broadcast on radio or television. You can also take the help of recorded material and use it on the tape-recorder.

The importance of listening has already been discussed. Only a good listener can be a good speaker. Reading fiction is also very important. It increases your vocabulary (word power). The most important feature of good fiction is the art of dramatic narration. The story is told through easy dialogues. So you can learn the art of dramatic narration.

Officers, executives, teachers and political leaders have to speak whether they like it or not. Public speaking can be made an enjoyable task if it is approached with due care and preparation. Skill in public speaking boosts your confidence. Self-confidence and self-esteem are the most important requirements of success.

## IMPORTANT STEPS FOR GOOD SPEAKING

(i) A speaker should have the right attitude. He should be willing to speak whenever he is required to do it.

(ii) In a speech the tone of voice, the choice of language and modulation of intonation are very important. The speaker should be careful about these things.

(iii) A good speaker does not overload his speech with facts and figures. He does not read from a prepared text. This will be boring to the audience and the speech will not be liked and appreciated.

(iv) Language has a charm, especially the spoken one. The speaker should speak in an inspiring manner and his speech should create a charm through lucidity of diction and spontaneity of expression.

# 22

# Words often Mis-spelt and Mis-Pronounced

The following is the list of some words commonly used in technical and business writing but are commonly misspelt.

A
Accede
Accept
Acceptable
Accessible
Accommodate
Accommodation
Accumulate
Achievement
Acquaint
Advantageous
Advisable
Align
Allege
Amateur
Antecedent
Apparatus
Application
Ascertain
Authorize
Auxiliary

B
Beginning
Beneficial
Benefited
Benevolent
Begin
Bilateral
Blueprint
Breakdown
Bureau
By-pass
By-product

C
Calendar
Cancel
Calibre
Cancellation
Career
Catalogue
Cautious

Changeable
Character
Characteristic
Commission
Commitment
Committed
Commodities
Companion
Compatibility
Competition
Concede
Concession
Conducive
Conscience
Conscientious
Consensus
Convenience
Co-operate
Coordinate
Cornerstone
Courteous
Courtesy

**D**
Debt
Debtor
Decision
Declaration
Deferred
Deficient
Depreciation
Discern
Discernible
Discrepancy
Dissolve
Divisible
Dubious

**E**
Eccentric
Economize
Economy
Eligible
Embarrass
Employee
Enrol
Ensure
Equipped
Erroneous
Exaggerate
Excess
Existence
Exorbitant
Expansion

**F**
Fantastic
Familiar
Feasible
Flexible
Foodstuff
Foolproof
Forbid
Forecast
Forfeit
Forgo
Fulfil

**G**
Gaudy
Generator
Generous
Grievance
Guarantee

**H**
Hallucination
Handicapped
Heterogeneous
Horror
Horrible
Horsepower
Hurriedly

**I**
Ignoble
Inadequate
Inconvenience
Indispensable
Inevitable
Innocent
Insist
Inspire
Install
Instalment
Instantaneous
Invariable
Irrelevant
Irresistible

**J**
Jeopardize
Judgement
Judicious
Justifiable

**K**
Kernel
Kingship
Keynote
Kilocycle
Kilometre
Knob
Knowledge

**L**
Lawyer
Legible
Liable
License
Lockout
Longevity
Loophole
Lucrative
Luscious

**M**
Magnificent
Magnify
Maintenance
Malpractice
Manageable
Mandatory
Manoeuvre
Manpower
Manufacture
Mediocre
Merchandise
Mileage
Miscellaneous
Misfire
Misinterpret
Misspell
Momentary

**N**
Native
Nationalize
Necessary
Nevertheless

Notepaper
Noteworthy
Noticeable
Notion
Notional
Nourishment

**O**

Obsolete
Occasion
Occasional
Occurred
Occurring
Official
Omission
Omitted
Opportunity
Originate
Overrule
Oversize
Overstate

**P**

Parallel
Partial
Percentage
Permissible
Persistence
Persuasion
Plausible
Possession
Practicable
Prevalent
Privilege
Procedure
Proceedings
Proficient
Proprietor
Provision

**Q**

Quest
Quarter
Questionnaire
Quorum
Quote

**R**

Rare
Rarely
Readjustment
Recede
Receipt
Receivable
Recipient
Reciprocal
Reciprocate
Reducible
Redundant
Reference
Regrettable
Reimbursement
Reinforce
Relevant
Remittance
Removal
Repetition
Replaceable
Requisition
Rhythm
Rudimentary

**S**

Sacred
Sacrifice

Safety valve
Salvage
Sanitary
Scarcely
Scarcity
Schedule
Seize
Sententious
Serviceable
Simultaneous
Sincerely
Spacious
Squeeze
Standardize
Straightforward
Subsidiary
Sufficient
Superintendent
Supersede
Supervise
Supervisor
Systematic

**T**
Tactfulness
Tangible
Technique
Tedious
Thoroughly
Trademark
Transferable
Treasurer
Turnover

**U**
Unbelievable
Unconscious
Uncontrollable
Undoubtedly
Unilateral
Unnecessary
Until
Usage
Usually

**V**
Vacant
Various
Variety
Versatile
Vicinity
Viewpoint
Volume

**W**
Warehouse
Warranted
Weight
Widespread
Witnessed
Worthwhile

**Y**
Yardstick
Yield

**Z**
Zigzag
Zealous

# 23

# One Word for Many

| | |
|---|---|
| A person who takes part in sports or other activities for pleasure and not for money. | Amateur |
| A situation where there is no order, law or control. | Anarchy |
| A name that is not known or not made public. | Anonymous |
| A person who is proud and shows little thought for other people. | Arrogant |
| A person who uses astrology to tell people about what might happen to them. | Astrologer |
| A person who does not believe that God exists. | Atheist |
| Group of people who gather to watch or listen something. | Audience |
| The story of a person's life written by himself. | Autobiography |
| A system of government of a country in which one person has complete power. | Autocracy |
| A person who has very strong unreasonable beliefs. | Bigot |

| | |
|---|---|
| One who cannot see | Blind |
| The system of official rules and ways of doing things in a government office. | Bureaucracy |
| A complete list of items. | Catalogue |
| One who designs and arranges steps in dancing. | Choreographer |
| A person that you work with in a profession or business. | Colleague |
| Belonging to the same time or to the present time. | Contemporary |
| Containing people of different types or from different places. | Cosmopolitan |
| A person who cannot hear. | Deaf |
| A person who cannot speak. | Dumb |
| Fit or suitable for eating. | Edible |
| A person who makes money by starting or running business involving financial risk. | Entrepreneur |
| Spoken or done without any previous thought or preparation. | Extempore |
| Being careful that every detail or something is correct. | Fastidious |
| One who believes that events are decided by fate. | Fatalist |
| A work /post without salary. | Honorary |
| What cannot be read. | Illegible |
| One who cannot read/write? | Illiterate |
| A plan which cannot be put into practice. | Impracticable |
| What cannot be heard? | Inaudible |
| What cannot be corrected? | Incorrigible |

| | |
|---|---|
| Impossible or very difficult to believe. | Incredible |
| A disease which cannot be cured. | Incurable |
| Never giving up or getting tired. | Indefatigable |
| That cannot be defended because it is morally unacceptable. | Indefensible |
| What cannot be divided? | Indivisible |
| One who does not meet the criteria of election or selection? | Ineligible |
| Impossible to forget or remove. | Indelible |
| Never doing wrong never making mistakes. | Infallible |
| Not allowed by the law. | Illegal |
| That cannot be understood or explained. | Inexplicable |
| A problem that cannot be solved. | Insoluble |
| One who has not enough money to pay what he owes. | Insolvent |
| What cannot be conquered? | Invincible |
| That cannot be copied. | Inimitable |
| What cannot be seen? | Invisible |
| Too important to be left out. | Indispensable |
| That cannot be harmed or defeated. | Invulnerable |
| What cannot be resisted or stopped. | Irresistible |
| A thing which cannot be repaired. | Irreparable |
| A person who knows several languages. | Linguist |
| Something that cannot be changed. | Irrevocable |
| A bird which migrates to other places. | Migratory |
| A copy of a book before it has been published. | Manuscript |

| | |
|---|---|
| The crime of killing one's mother | Matricide |
| Having total power, able to do everything. | Omnipotent |
| Present everywhere. | Omnipresent |
| A person who always expects good things to happen. | Optimist |
| To make something illegal. | Outlaw |
| A person who is able to tell future after looking at the palms of somebody. | Palmist |
| Unable to move because suffering from paralysis. | Paralytic |
| A person who always relies on or benefits from other people. | Parasite |
| A person walking in a street (not travelling in a vehicle). | Pedestrian |
| A person who always expects bad things to happen. | Pessimist |
| A rich person who helps the poor people and those in need. | Philanthropist |
| A person who studies or writes about philosophy. | Philosopher |
| An excuse or explanation that is reasonable/likely to be true. | Plausible |
| The custom of having more than one wife at the same time. | Polygamy |
| Medical examination of a dead body | Postmortem |
| Happening, done, published after a persons has died. | Posthumous |
| A person who is unwilling to tell persons about things. | Reticent |
| A country that is governed by politicians elected by people. | Republic |

| | |
|---|---|
| A person who is watching especially a sports event. | Spectator |
| A person who speaks on behalf of a group or organization. | Spokesperson |
| The act of killing oneself. | Suicide |
| Happening at the same time. | Simultaneously |
| An opinion or decision agreed or shared by everyone. | Unanimously |
| That cannot be destroyed, defeated of questioned. | Unassailable |
| Impossible to avoid or prevent. | Unavoidable |
| That cannot be obtained. | Unavailable |
| What cannot be understood? | Unintelligible |
| Not friendly, not enjoying company of other people. | Unsociable |
| A person who shows where to sit in a church, hall. | Usher |
| A person who does not eat meat or fish. | Vegetarian |
| A person who has a lot of experience in a particular area or activity. | Veteran |

# 24

# Synonyms and Antonyms

| Words | Synonyms |
|---|---|
| **A** | |
| Abandon | Forsake, give up |
| Abate | Decrease, subside |
| Abdicate | Relinquish |
| Abduct | Kidnap |
| Abhor | Hate |
| Ability | Skill, competence |
| Abject | Wretched, pitiful |
| Able | Capable |
| Abnormal | Unusual |
| Abrupt | Sudden |
| Abstain | Refrain |
| Abundant | Plentiful |
| Accelerate | Hasten |
| Accident | Mishap |
| Accomplish | Fulfil |
| Ache | Pain |
| Acquit | Release |
| Adapt | Adjust |

| | |
|---|---|
| Adept | Expert |
| Admirable | Commendable |
| Adore | Worship |
| Agile | Quick |
| Agony | Pain |
| Aid | Assist |
| Alert | Cautious |
| Allow | Permit |
| Allude | Suggest |
| Ally | Associate |
| Alter | Change |
| Altitude | Height |
| Amass | Accumulate |
| Ambiguous | Unclear |
| Ample | Sufficient |
| Amuse | Entertain |
| Announce | Declare |
| Antipathy | Aversion |
| Appeal | Entreaty |
| Appease | Pacify |
| Appreciate | Esteem |
| Arid | Dry |
| Arrest | Apprehend |
| Arrogance | Haughtiness |
| Ascend | Climb |
| Attachment | Devotion |
| Auspicious | Fortunate |
| Aversion | Dislike |

| | |
|---|---|
| **B** | |
| Beautiful | Attractive |
| Bliss | Happiness |
| Bloom | Blossom |
| Bottom | Base |
| Bright | Brilliant, dazzling |
| Bureau | Department |
| **C** | |
| Capacity | Capability |
| Celebrity | Star |
| Cheer | Applause |
| Cheerful | Happy |
| Chivalrous | Heroic |
| Clamour | Uproar |
| Clemency | Mercy |
| Colossal | Enormous |
| Comely | Attractive |
| Conceal | Hide |
| Correct | Accurate |
| Credit | Acclaim |
| **D** | |
| Despair | Hopelessness |
| Despise | Hate |
| Difficult | Hard |
| Dignified | Stately |
| Disadvantage | Inconvenience |
| Disclose | Reveal |
| Discord | Conflict |
| Distinct | Peculiar |

| | |
|---|---|
| Distinguished | Celebrated |
| Dry | Arid |
| Dull | Uninteresting |
| **E** | |
| Ecstasy | Delight |
| Effective | Productive |
| Elementary | Primary |
| Eloquent | Articulate |
| Emancipate | Liberate |
| Emphasis | Stress |
| Endure | Tolerate |
| Enhance | Increase |
| Enough | Sufficient |
| Environment | Surroundings |
| Episode | Event |
| Equanimity | Poise |
| Eradicate | Eliminate |
| Erroneous | Mistaken |
| Esteem | Respect |
| Estimate | Assess |
| Evidence | Proof |
| Excellent | Superb |
| Except | Barring |
| Exchange | Transact |
| Exile | Banish |
| Explore | Investigate |
| Exquisite | Elegant |
| Extent | Limit |
| Extreme | Utmost |
| Exult | Rejoice |

| F | |
|---|---|
| Fabulous | Fantastic |
| Faction | Group |
| Factual | Accurate |
| Fair | Just, impartial |
| Faith | Trust |
| Faithful | Loyal |
| Faithless | Disloyal |
| Fake | False |
| Falsehood | Untruth |
| Familiar | Well known |
| Fanatical | Extremist |
| Fantastic | Amazing |
| Fantasy | Dream, illusion |
| Fascinate | Attract, charm |
| Fast | Quick |
| Fastidious | Meticulous |
| Fatal | Disastrous |
| Faulty | Defective |
| Feasible | Possible |
| Feat | Performance |
| Feeble | Weak |
| Feign | Pretend |
| Fellowship | Comradeship |
| Ferocious | Savage, violent |
| Fictitious | Imaginary |
| Fidelity | Loyalty |
| Flamboyant | Gaudy |
| Flaw | Defect |
| Fluent | Eloquent |

| | |
|---|---|
| Foe | Enemy |
| Fondness | Liking |
| Forecast | Predict |
| Formidable | Overwhelming |
| Frailty | Weakness |
| Fret | Worry |
| Futile | Pointless |
| **G** | |
| Gaiety | Merriment |
| Gain | Profit |
| Gloomy | Depressing |
| Graceful | Elegant |
| Guilty | Convicted |
| **H** | |
| Habitation | Dwelling |
| Hamper | Hinder |
| Hardships | Difficulties |
| Hardy | Sturdy |
| Harm | Injury |
| Harmful | Injurious |
| Headstrong | Obstinate |
| Honesty | Truthfulness |
| Humility | Modesty |
| Humorous | Amusing |
| Hush | Silence |
| **I** | |
| Illegible | Unreadable |
| Illogical | Unreasonable |
| Imaginary | Fictitious |
| Immaterial | Unimportant |

| | |
|---|---|
| Immoral | Unethical |
| Immortal | Eternal |
| Impartial | Unbiased |
| Imperceptible | Unnoticeable |
| Impartial | Unbiased |
| Inaccessible | Unreachable |
| Include | Incorporate |
| Inconsistent | Unsteady |
| Infinite | Limitless |
| Issue | Copy, edition |
| **J** | |
| Judicious | Prudent |
| Justice | Fairness |
| Justification | Reason |
| Justify | Defend |
| **K** | |
| Keen | Sharp |
| Kidnap | Abduct |
| Kin | Relative |
| Kindness | Benevolence |
| Knack | Ability |
| Knave | Rogue |
| **L** | |
| Lad | Boy |
| Languid | Weak |
| Lasting | Durable |
| Least | Minimum |
| Liberal | Generous |
| Likely | Probable |
| Lucky | Fortunate |

| **M** | |
|---|---|
| Magnify | Enlarge |
| Manageable | Controllable |
| Manly | Brave |
| Marvellous | Wonderful |
| Maxim | Proverb |
| Meek | Gentle |
| Miserable | Wretched |
| Modest | Humble |
| Mount | Climb |
| Mysterious | Strange |
| **N** | |
| Necessary | Essential |
| Notion | Idea |
| Notorious | Infamous |
| Nourish | Feed |
| Nutritious | Healthy |
| Nymph | Fairy |
| **O** | |
| Odious | Hateful |
| Order | Command |
| Ordinary | Commonplace |
| Ostentatious | Pretentious |
| Outset | Beginning |
| Outward | Exterior |
| Overlook | Neglect |
| Overt | Obvious |
| Own | Possess |

| | |
|---|---|
| **P** | |
| Paradise | Heaven |
| Paramount | Chief |
| Partial | Incomplete |
| Particular | Specific |
| Partition | Division |
| Passion | Fervour |
| Peerless | Incomparable |
| Perfect | Flawless |
| Pertinent | Appropriate |
| Pine | Yearn |
| Pleasant | Pleasing |
| Plenty | Abundant |
| Polite | Courteous |
| Primitive | Ancient |
| Profit | Gain |
| Profound | Deep |
| Prosaic | Common |
| Prudent | Discerning |
| **Q** | |
| Quiet | Silent |
| Quiver | Tremble |
| Quota | Portion |
| **R** | |
| Rare | Uncommon |
| Rational | Reasonable |
| Recollect | Remember |
| Recover | Recuperate |
| Refined | Cultured |
| Relevant | Appropriate |

| | |
|---|---|
| Relinquish | Forego |
| Reluctance | Unwillingness |
| Remedy | Cure |
| Remit | Pay |
| Remuneration | Payment |
| Renown | Fame |
| Repugnant | Repulsive |
| Reticent | Taciturn |
| Retreat | Withdraw |
| Reward | Prize |
| Right | Correct |
| **S** | |
| Scanty | Meager |
| Scold | Reprove |
| Sensitive | Tender |
| Shortage | Deficiency |
| Significant | Important |
| Silly | Foolish |
| Similar | Alike |
| Slander | Defame |
| Social | Friendly |
| Sort | Kind |
| Spectacle | Sight |
| Spendthrift | Prodigal |
| Spoil | Damage |
| Startle | Surprise |
| Stately | Majestic |
| Steady | Consistent |
| Sterile | Barren |
| Stormy | Turbulent |

| | |
|---|---|
| Sullen | Gloomy |
| Surmise | Guess |
| Suspicious | Doubtful |
| Symbol | Sign |
| **T** | |
| Taboo | Banned |
| Taciturn | Quiet |
| Tale | Story |
| Tame | Domesticate |
| Temper | Disposition |
| Tedious | Boring |
| Terminate | End |
| Thrash | Beat |
| Threaten | Intimidate |
| Thrift | Frugality |
| Tolerable | Bearable |
| Tragedy | Calamity |
| Trait | Quality |
| Transcend | Surmount |
| Transient | Transitory |
| Transmit | Communicate |
| Transparent | Clear |
| Treason | Sedition |
| Tuition | Coaching |
| Tumultuous | Disorderly |
| Tyrant | Oppressor |
| **U** | |
| Ugly | Unattractive |
| Ultimate | Final |
| Unassuming | Modest |

| | |
|---|---|
| Understand | Comprehend |
| Unruffled | Unperturbed |
| Unwholesome | Unhealthy |
| Unwieldy | Awkward |
| Usual | Customary |
| Utter | Speak |
| **V** | |
| Vain | Futile |
| Valiant | Brave |
| Vanish | Disappear |
| Veto | Reject |
| Vicinity | Surroundings |
| Vigilant | Alert |
| Vigour | Strength |
| Virtue | Righteousness |
| Vivacious | Lively |
| Vivid | Clear |
| **W** | |
| Wage | Earnings |
| Wail | Moan |
| Wander | Roam |
| War | Battle |
| Warn | Caution |
| Wary | Cautious |
| Waterfall | Cascade |
| Worthy | Deserving |
| **Y** | |
| Yearn | Crave |
| Yell | Scream |
| Yoke | Bondage |

| | |
|---|---|
| **Z** | |
| Zeal | Enthusiasm |
| Zenith | Summit |
| Zest | Passion |
| Zone | Region |

## ANTONYMS

| Words | Antonyms |
|---|---|
| **A** | |
| Abate | Increase |
| Abbreviate | Expand |
| Ability | Inability |
| Abnormal | Normal |
| Above | Below |
| Absence | Presence |
| Abstract | Concrete |
| Accept | Reject |
| Accidental | Deliberate |
| Accord | Discord |
| Acquit | Convict |
| Active | Inactive |
| Add | Subtract |
| Advantage | Disadvantage |
| Adversity | Prosperity |
| Advisable | Inadvisable |
| Agree | Disagree |
| Aimless | Purposeful |
| Amateur | Professional |
| Ambiguous | Plain, clear |
| Ample | Insufficient |

| | |
|---|---|
| Ancient | Modern |
| Aptitude | Inaptitude |
| Arrival | Departure |
| Artificial | Real |
| Attentive | Inattentive |
| Attract | Repulse |
| Auspicious | Inauspicious |
| Available | Unavailable |
| Awful | Elegant |
| **B** | |
| Beautiful | Ugly |
| Begin | End |
| Bitter | Sweet |
| Bright | Dull |
| Brutal | Humane |
| Buy | Sell |
| **C** | |
| Capacity | Incapacity |
| Captivity | Liberty |
| Careless | Careful |
| Cheerful | Sad |
| Civil | Uncivil |
| Colossal | Tiny |
| Commence | Conclude |
| Conceal | Reveal |
| Confidence | Diffidence |
| Considerate | Inconsiderate |
| Courtesy | Discourtesy |
| Credit | Discredit |
| Crude | Refined |

| | |
|---|---|
| **D** | |
| Dark | Bright |
| Decent | Indecent |
| Deep | Shallow |
| Defeat | Win |
| Demise | Birth |
| Detach | Attach |
| Diffident | Bold |
| Disadvantage | Advantage |
| Disclose | Conceal |
| Discomfort | Comfort |
| Distinct | Indistinct |
| Dry | Wet |
| Dull | Bright |
| **E** | |
| Edible | Inedible |
| Eject | Retain |
| Elastic | Rigid |
| Employ | Dismiss |
| Encourage | Discourage |
| Enemy | Friend |
| Erect | Demolish |
| Ethereal | Earthly |
| Exhale | Inhale |
| External | Internal |
| **F** | |
| Fact | Fiction |
| Fail | Succeed |
| Failure | Success |
| Fake | Real |

| | |
|---|---|
| Fashionable | Unfashionable |
| Fondness | Dislike |
| Foolish | Sensible |
| Forceful | Weak |
| Formal | Informal |
| Fortunate | Unfortunate |
| Forward | Backward |
| Frailty | Strength |
| Freedom | Slavery |
| Future | Past |
| **G** | |
| Gaiety | Gloom |
| Gain | Loss |
| Gloomy | Cheerful |
| Graceful | Graceless |
| Guilty | Innocent |
| **H** | |
| Hardy | Frail |
| Harmful | Harmless |
| Honesty | Dishonesty |
| Honour | Dishonour |
| Hopeful | Hopeless |
| Humble | Proud |
| Hurry | Dally |
| Hush | Silence |
| Hypocrisy | Sincerity |
| **I** | |
| Illegal | Legal |
| Illegible | Legible |
| Illiterate | Literate |

| | |
|---|---|
| Immature | Mature |
| Immoral | Moral |
| Impartial | Partial |
| Important | Unimportant |
| Improper | Proper |
| Include | Exclude |
| Competent | Incompetent |
| Infinite | Finite |
| Insanity | Sanity |
| Irregular | Regular |
| **J** | |
| Judicious | Injudicious |
| Justice | Injustice |
| Justify | Accuse |
| **K** | |
| Keen | Blunt |
| Kind | Unkind |
| Knack | Ineptitude |
| **L** | |
| Lawful | Unlawful |
| Least | Most |
| Liberal | Illiberal |
| Liberate | Enslave |
| Light | Heavy, dark |
| Likely | Unlikely |
| Loose | Tight |
| Lucky | Unlucky |
| Luminous | Dim |
| Luxuriant | Sparse |

| | |
|---|---|
| **M** | |
| Manageable | Unmanageable |
| Manly | Cowardly |
| Master | Servant |
| Meaningless | Meaningful |
| Meek | Assertive |
| Melancholy | Joyful |
| Miser | Spendthrift |
| Miserable | Happy |
| Mobile | Immobile |
| Modest | Proud |
| Mount | Dismount |
| **N** | |
| Natural | Unnatural |
| Necessary | Unnecessary |
| Normal | Abnormal |
| Notice | Overlook |
| Notorious | Famous |
| Numerous | Few |
| Nutritious | Unhealthy |
| **O** | |
| Obey | Disobey |
| Obnoxious | Charming |
| Obscure | Clear |
| Odious | Admirable |
| Open | Close |
| Order | Disorder |
| Ordinary | Extraordinary |
| Outward | Inward |

| | |
|---|---|
| Overt | Covert |
| Own | Disown |
| **P** | |
| Paradise | Hell |
| Partial | Impartial |
| Partly | Wholly |
| Passive | Active |
| Peace | War |
| Peak | Bottom |
| Perfect | Imperfect |
| Personal | Impersonal |
| Persuade | Dissuade |
| Pleasant | Unpleasant |
| Plentiful | Scanty |
| Polite | Impolite |
| Poor | Rich |
| Possible | Impossible |
| Poverty | Richness |
| Primitive | Modern |
| Profit | Loss |
| Prudent | Imprudent |
| Pure | Impure |
| **Q** | |
| Quick | Slow |
| Quiet | Noisy |
| **R** | |
| Rare | Common |
| Rational | Irrational |
| Reasonable | Unreasonable |
| Recollect | Forget |

| | |
|---|---|
| Refined | Coarse |
| Relevant | Irrelevant |
| Religious | Irreligious |
| Reluctance | Willingness |
| Responsible | Irresponsible |
| Reveal | Conceal |
| Rich | Poor |
| Right | Wrong |
| **S** | |
| Sacred | Profane |
| Sane | Insane |
| Scanty | Plentiful |
| Senseless | Sensible |
| Significant | Insignificant |
| Strength | Weakness |
| Sullen | Cheerful |
| Sweet | Bitter |
| Swift | Slow |
| **T** | |
| Tight | Loose |
| Tolerable | Intolerable |
| Trifle | Significant |
| Truth | Falsehood |
| **U** | |
| Ugly | Beautiful |
| Unfortunate | Fortunate |
| Untidy | Tidy |
| **V** | |
| Virtue | Vice |
| Vivid | Vague |

| | |
|---|---|
| Voluntary | Compulsory |
| Vulnerable | Invulnerable |
| **W** | |
| Warm | Cold |
| Worthy | Unworthy |
| Wrong | Right |
| **Y** | |
| Yell | Whisper |
| Young | Old |
| Youth | Adult |
| Youthful | Aged |
| **Z** | |
| Zeal | Apathy |
| Zealous | Dispassionate |
| Zenith | Nadir |

# 25

# Seminar Presentation

## WHAT IS SEMINAR PRESENTATION?

A "seminar" is a meeting for discussion or training. In the academic sphere a seminar is a class at a university or a college where a small group of students and a teacher discuss a particular topic. Presentation is the way in which something is offered, shown or explained. A seminar is an informal talk about your findings or research. So a seminar presentation can be defined as a small group of persons in a class or in an organization assembled to have an exchange of views on a particular topic. The participants express their views on the given topic in an informal way. So a seminar is a very enlightening and effective information sharing process. Holding of a seminar is a teaching learning process.

## IMPORTANCE OF SEMINARS/ADVANTAGES OF SEMINARS

Seminars offer opportunities for fair and free discussion on a given topic. Participants express their views in a systematic and analytical way so that each aspect of the topic is thoroughly discussed. In the modern world characterized by fast industrial growth and sophistication in business management techniques ability to present your views is highly desirable and it is appreciated by business houses.

At the academic level seminars hone the presentation skills of the students as they learn and practise the basic techniques of presentation. Speaking well in a seminar improves your presentation skills to make you competent to face the challenges of leadership in an organization. Through training and practice you learn the skills of presenting your ideas logically and to report the results of your research, investigation or enquiry. By effective presentation you can convince your audience about the veracity of what you speak or plan to do. Through methodical training and practice you can learn how to make your presentation interesting, engaging and informative.

## HOW CAN YOU MAKE AN EFFECTIVE PRESENTATION?

(1) The most important thing is the preparation to be made about the seminar. You should have a good fundamental knowledge of the subject. It will enable you to speak with confidence as well as to enable you to answer satisfactorily the questions put to you.

(2) Write, plan and organize your material so that your presentation has a logical progression. A well-planned presentation has:

   (i) Introduction of the topic
   (ii) Explanation of the subject matter
   (iii) Conclusion

Introduction of the topic is very important. It can arrest the attention of the audience. It becomes enthusiastic about your presentation. Before giving the introduction of the topic you may greet the audience and introduce yourself. You may start your presentation by asking a question. Suppose your topic is the importance of computers - you can ask. "Would you like to live in a world without computers?" or "Can you imagine today's world without computers?"

## THE MAIN BODY

After introducing the subject of the seminar you should elaborate the subject in a logical and coherent way. Your presentation must have:

(i) Clarity of expression
(ii) Accuracy of language
(iii) Spontaneity of expression

## CONCLUSION

In the concluding part you should give a summary of the whole presentation. You should give solutions of the problems discussed and suggestions, if any. Don't forget to thank the audience for listening to your presentation attentively and with interest.

## IMPORTANT FEATURES OF GOOD SEMINAR PRESENTATION

(i) The first thing the audience notice is the dress and appearance. It is said that dress proclaims the man. Dress yourself well for your seminar presentation. It does not mean that you should wear gaudy and expensive clothes. Your dress should be complete, simple and neat and clean. If you are wearing a shirt, wear a neck-tie also. You should wear shoes and not chappals or sandals.

(ii) **Body language:** While presenting your seminar do not stand like a statue. Let your eyes and face also speak. You should express your ideas as much through your facial expressions as you do through your language.

(iii) Maintain your eye contact with your audience so that they feel they are getting due attention from you.

(iv) Do not make a speech but talk to your audience.

(v) **Remain Cheerful and positive:** Your cheerfulness and positive attitude will help you a lot. Cheerfulness is infectious. It moves from you to your audience. If you are cheerful your audience will never feel bored and your presentation will never be dull.

(vi) Speak at a very slow speed but loudly enough for your audience to listen to you.

(vii) English is a rhythm based language, modulate your voice giving suitable pauses.

The above-mentioned steps will help you to do well in seminars and group discussions.

## TOPICS FOR SEMINAR PRESENTATION

(1) Life without computers
(2) Television - a blessing or a curse
(3) How to obtain the wholehearted cooperation of the work force?
(4) The importance of discipline in business career.

# 26

# Group Discussions

## WHAT IS A GROUP DISCUSSION?

Group discussions provide a platform to a group of persons for discussion on a given subject. They are designed to judge the knowledge of participants on the given subject as well as to judge their presentation skills. They are organized to judge how efficiently and effectively people judge each other's ideas. Group discussions are meant to judge the ability of the participants to resolve their professional differences which result in success or failure.

A group discussion assesses the capacity of a person to interact effectively as a member of a group. It assesses whether you can make a meaningful contribution to the discussion.

## IMPORTANCE OF GROUP DISCUSSIONS

Group discussions play an important role in the recruitment process. They have become an essential feature of recruitment process. Business organizations organize group discussions for recruitment for administrative and high level posts. Nowadays group discussions have also become a part of the admission process in institutes of higher education.

## KEY TO SUCCESS IN GROUP DISCUSSIONS

(1) You can do very well in group discussions if you have a good knowledge base.

(2) You have the ability to present your arguments logically.

(3) You have the ability to communicate your ideas very convincingly. Moreover, presenting your ideas plainly and simply is of great advantage. Skill in interpersonal communication can help you a lot.

## TYPES OF GROUP DISCUSSIONS

1. In the first type of group discussion a topic is given by the coordinator. Participants are asked to discuss the topic for 15 to 20 minutes. Sometimes the coordinator asks the participants to choose the topic themselves. In that case the participants are given 4/5 minutes to choose the topic after which the group discussion starts.
2. In the second type of group discussion the participants are given a printed case study. They are given some time to read the case before the discussion begins. In this type of group discussion the participants are advised to follow the procedure given below:
   (i) Study and analyse the facts of the case.
   (ii) Identify the problems.
   (iii) Suggest solutions.
   (iv) Be assertive but not aggressive.
   (v) Convey your ideas logically and convincingly.
   (vi) Avoid verbosity, i.e., do not use more words than required.
   (vii) Give examples to substantiate your viewpoint.
   (viii) In a group discussion language should be polite and friendly.
   (ix) Be a good listener, listen attentively to the other speakers.

(x) Do not interfere with the other speakers.

(xi) Summarize the discussion at the end.

(xii) Use the proper body language like eye contact to show your interest in the discussion.

(xiii) Be positive and remain cheerful throughout the discussion.

(xiv) Thank the moderators before leaving the hall.

(xv) Before joining the discussion write down the important points of the topic.

## ABILITIES THAT THE EVALUATORS LOOK FOR IN THE PARTICIPANTS

(i) Intelligent grasp of the subject.

(ii) The depth of understanding.

(iii) Ability of the participants to articulate their thoughts.

(iv) Ability to relate to other people and ability to appreciate the point of view of other speakers.

(v) Command over spoken language – the ability to present your viewpoint logically, coherently and appropriately in simple and correct English and ability to modulate the voice.

(vi) Body language – the ability to use body language corresponding with the expression of thoughts.

### Here are some helpful lines for group discussions

(i) In my view ...

(ii) I believe.....

(iii) It is obvious.....

(iv) I tend to think.....

### Expressing Agreement

(i) I think you are right .....

(ii) I agree entirely .....

(iii) I totally agree....

(iv) I think the approach is right ....

### Making a suggestion

(i) Perhaps we should ....

(ii) It might be worth .....

(iii) What about .....

(iv) I suggest that .....

### Expressing disagreement

(i) I'm afraid I can't agree with what you say...

(ii) I don't agree at all,

(iii) I don't really think so .....

(iv) I think differently on this point ....

Even while expressing disagreement the language should be polite and attitude friendly.

# 27

# Job Interviews

An interview is a formal meeting at which candidates are asked questions by the members of the interview board to see if they are suitable for a particular job or for a course of study at a college, university etc. It is a face-to-face interaction of a candidate with the members of the board for the purpose of judging the depth of knowledge and personal traits of the candidate. The objective of an interview is to check the suitability and eligibility of the candidate for the particular post. Employers want to select the most suitable person for the specific job. Selection of a wrong candidate can create problems.

## IMPORTANCE OF INTERVIEWS

Successful performance in an interview is important for admission in a course of study. It is also important for securring a job in an organization or government office. The employment procedure for a high ranking post is written test followed by an interview. For some higher posts in industry and business organizations the basis of recruitment is solely the interview.

## PREPARATION FOR THE INTERVIEW

Success in an interview requires a lot of preparation. There is a short term preparation and a long term preparation. A judicious person plans his/her career and starts preparation for it in his/her school or college days. If he/she wants to be an electrical engineer he/she makes a detailed study of this subject to become master of it but he/she also tries to know something about related subjects. He/she is supposed to know everything of something and something of everything. He/she should read newspapers regularly to keep abreast of what is happening in the world. Moreover, reading of newspapers broadens one's outlook and gives a broader vision.

For short term preparations go through the copy of your application before the interview. The interview board may ask specific questions about it.

## APPEARANCE

When you appear for an interview the first impression is created by your dress. It is said that dress proclaims the man. Be decently dressed. Your dress should be complete, neat and clean. If you are wearing a suit, it must be accompanied with a neck-tie. You must wear well-polished shoes.

Seek permission to enter the room. Greet the members by saying Good Morning, Sirs. Good evening, Sirs. Sit only when asked to sit and thank the members after taking your seat.

Your success in the interview largely depends on your attitude.

## SOME TIPS FOR THE INTERVIEW

(i) You must have a lot of confidence in yourself.

(ii) Remaining cheerful is a very positive attitude.

(iii) Never get irritated even if you are asked some awkward questions.

(iv) Ask questions if something is not clear to you.

(v) Be open and honest. Don't try to bluff. The members of the board are wise enough to know the truth. Once you lose your integrity, you are lost. If you don't know an answer, politely say "I am sorry, Sir. I don't know". You are not expected to know each and everything in the world.

(vi) Be careful about non-verbal clues, such as eye-contact, posture, gestures etc.

(vii) Be as natural as you can.

(viii) Show enthusiasm and interest.

(ix) Listening attentively is very important. If you do not understand anything, say "Pardon sir".

Giving what you have is not important. To give what the company wants is important. So try to find out what the company expects from you and try to give it.

## PROBABLE INTERVIEW QUESTIONS

**(i)** **Introduce yourself:** The companies want to know a lot about you. They start with the question about your personal life to make you feel comfortable and easy. You should be able to tell everything about yourself.

**(ii)** **Your greatest strengths:** They may ask you about your strengths. If you are competent in resolving conflicts tell them about this.

**(iii)** **Your weaknesses:** If you are aware of some of your weaknesses admit them frankly. You will present the image of an honest, frank and straightforward person.

**(iv)** They may ask you as to why you want to work for them. Explain the reasons for your interest in the company. You can create a very good impression by highlighting the achievements of the company and by pointing out that it would be a great privilege for you to be associated with such a renowned company.

Finally, you may be asked subject specific questions – asking questions about the subjects you have studied.

Try to explain whatever you are asked. Explain with the help of examples and illustrations.

When the interview is over thank the members of the board before leaving the room.